The History of Cooch Behar State Force

A Study of the Glorious Period

The History of Cooch Behar State Force

A Study of the Glorious Period

Joydeep Pal

ABHIJEET PUBLICATIONS
NEW DELHI 110002

ABHIJEET PUBLICATIONS
4658-A, First Floor, Ambika Bhawan,
21 Ansari Road, New Delhi 110002
Phone: 011-23259444
E-mail: abhijeetpublication@gmail.com
twitter:- @AbhijeetPub21
whatsapp:- 8076785356
Facebook:- https://www.facebook.com/abhijeetpublications
instagram: @abhijeet_publications
LinkedIn: jitendra-singh-7729292b/
Website: www.abhijeetpublications.com

THE HISTORY OF COOCH BEHAR STATE FORCE: A STUDY OF THE GLORIOUS PERIOD

First Published 2022

ISBN 978-93-92816-12-3

PRINTED IN INDIA

Published by J.K. Singh for Abhijeet Publications, New Delhi-110002, Lasertypeset by Abhijeet Typesetters, New Delhi and Printed at Milan Enterprises, New Delhi.

IN

MEMORY

OF

MY

MOTHER

Late Krishna De Sarkar (Pal)

(***who is there, who is not***)

Preface

Before going to discuss on the proposed study, which is the 22nd one (book) in my short academic career as a writer (as a sole author), I would like to write a few lines on my mother. As a writer or as a scholar I have done a number of works under the guidance of my mother (friend, philosopher and guide in my day to day life). In this connection here it must be include that my mother Late Smt. Krishna De Sarkar (Pal) was a multi-talented women. She was a Classical singer in the field of music, a true academician specially (in psychology, Sanskrit, Hindi) in the field of education, a consistent learner in teaching–learning process, a book-lover (she had a collection of enormous Epic books), a Fabric Painting Artist, An Industrially trained dress designer, a social worker (who spent time for the welfare of women), a broad-minded, soft spoken, fun-loving women, who always ready to extent economic help to poor and needy persons whatever possible for her and she was also a gardener (nourishing various flowers, fruits and vegetables). Her departure (abruptly) will remain as an unrecoverable injury for the rest of my life as an unlucky one (as an unlucky single child).

When I am selecting such kind of topic, at first I went to discuss it with my mother and she inspired me with her valuable suggestions. Without her suggestions at the initial stages its quite impossible for me to sum up the issue. Such an issue started its preliminary frame work under her guidance.

History is a full of documentation which are inter-linked with one another. If history explain always through the process of explanation, then it can be say that history may evolve new chapters of the glorious past. The history of the Princely State is an example of history of a native place which help the people to understand the importance of the particular State and at the same time it play the role of an autobiography of a State i.e. the contribution of the rulers towards the kingdom. In India most of the Princely States got the opportunity of modernity mean western culture, when they came under the shadow of the Colonial rulers. But most of them could not contribute much in the welfare of the State. When Cooch Behar came in contact with the British, the rulers took the good things of the western culture and injected it in the moderation of the State. Here it need to mention that the State of Cooch Behar had a history of its own which is around 450 years of old.

An attempt has been made in the present work to discuss in detail manner the various avenues of the State force. From Ancient to Modern times history provide a lot of example of structured administrative system of the Princely States. Cooch Behar is not an exception to that. Situated in the north–eastern frontier of India this State set an example of modern means of force system. The rulers of the State were out and out modern in their outlook. They took their education in England but as a product of the East, they implemented various economic measures in the modernization of State of Cooch Behar. Historical analysis of such an issue was a tough work for the writer. Cooch Behar State got all sorts of economic stability during the rule of the welfare rulers.

The aspect of State force is a distinct feature, because it shows the well furnished system in the State. If any researcher thoroughly investigate the history of settlement operations in the Princely State of Cooch Behar, he can find that under the ruling dynasty such an issue gained momentum since 1870's with the accession of Maharaja Nripendra Narayan on the throne of Cooch Behar. His father Maharaja Narendra Narayan did a commendable job in this field, who initiated the process.

Here it need to mention that due to lack of authentic source material Annual Administration Reports of the Cooch Behar State play a dominant role in writing the glorious history of the Princely State of Cooch Behar.

Joydeep Pal

Acknowledgements

The difficult task, for a researcher, is to acknowledge his indebtedness to all of them who took part in one way or the other, in shaping his thought process and ideas, rather difficult to mention all of them by name. However, it is imperative to express my gratitude to them who are directly and indirectly associated with this study.

First of all, I must express a deep sense of gratitude to Late Professor Jasobanta Kar, for his eminently, scholarly, meticulous and inspiring guidance – a constant source of inspiration and encouragement and progress of this work.

I am also indebted to Professor Chhanda Chakraborty (former), Department of History, University of North Bengal, encouraged me by valuable suggestions and relevant sources from her own collections.

I also recall Professor Ratna Roy (Sanyal), {(former) Department of History, University of North Bengal}, Dr. Nilangshu Sekhar Das ,Principal, Sukanta Mahavidyalaya, Professor

Suresh Jnaneswaran, Dean of Faculty of Social Sciences, University of Kerala, showed their interest for this work by rendering few rare sources connected with this work. It was really a rare opportunity for me to develop my idea with a comparative view and knowledge about this work.

My heartfelt thanks to Professor Nirban Basu, Department of History, University of Calcutta have ever shown his interest and extended academic help whatever possible for him.

Thanks are due to my childhood friends, colleagues for their constant help, inspiration and mental support in this academic venture.

Sources have not always been easy to find, but my labours have been eased by the courtesy of the staff of the following libraries: National Library (Kolkata), West Bengal State Archive-s (Kolkata), National Archives (New Delhi), Nehru Memorial Museum and Library (New Delhi), North Bengal State Library (Cooch Behar), University of North Bengal's Library.

Needless to mention, no words will be adequate to express my gratitude to the members of my family who have stood by me over these long testing times in the accomplishment of my study.

Joydeep Pal

Contents

Abbreviations

Annual Administration Report of Cooch Behar State	——	A.A.R. of the C.B.S.
The Cooch Behar Darpan	——	T.C.B.D.
West Bengal District Gazetteers (Koch Behar)	——	W.B.D.G (Koch Behar)

Glossary

Ahilkar	–	Officer.
Amla	–	Royal servant.
Anna	–	Rupee.
Bhote	–	Sharp-less.
Cheker	–	Checker.
Chekwar	–	Checker.
Chora	–	knife.
Chowki	–	Wooden Rectangular Bed.
Chowkidar	–	Guard.
Cooli	–	Labour.
Cutcha	–	Revenue department.
Dewan	–	Prime Minister.
Dewani	–	Civil.
Fouzdari		Criminal.
Hajut	–	Custody.
Jamadar	–	Record keeper.
Kacha	–	raw material.
Khas	–	Royal Land.

Kucha	–	Temporary.
Mahajans	–	money lenders.
Maunds	–	measure.
Mensem	–	count of distance.
Mistrees	–	Mason.
Mohurrirs	–	Land record writers.
Mora	–	Stool.
Mufussil	–	Town.
Munshif	–	Lawyer.
Naib	–	Deputy Prime Minister.
Nazir	–	Commander in Chief.
Nullahs	–	Drainage.
Pucca	–	Concrete.
Sataranch	–	Mat.
Sheristadar	–	Household keeper.
Soorkee	–	small pieces of bricks.
Taluk	–	Small unit of village.
Thana	–	Police Station.
Turkarees	–	Vegetables.

Introduction

On the subject of General administration some notable features has been visible during the rule of the Maharaja's of Cooch Behar State. In this matter first of all it can be said that the Colonial Government of Lord Cornwallis appointed Lawrence Mercer and Jhon Lewis Chauvet as Commissioners to report on various subjects including the mode in which the British influence should be exercised for better administration of the State in future. The earliest knowledge about the internal administration of Cooch Behar State comes from the report of Mercer and Chauvet dated December 10, 1788.[1]

Here it need to mention that at that time i.e in 1788 era there was only one court in Cooch Behar for the trial of all kinds of cases. The Court exercised powers in the name of Maharaja of Cooch Behar. Written petitions were received by the Court presided over by Sivaprasad Mustafi which held public sittings at the palace.[2] The petitions were placed before the Maharaja and with his approval summonses were issued to the parties who after appearance were bound over by bonds. The cases and causes were determined in accordance with the Common Hindu Law enjoined in the Smirits, the law on the relevant matters being propounded by the Pandit of the Court. The order of the Court was placed before the Maharaja. There were no fixed dates for the sittings of the Court and except for revenue matters the records were not preserved.[3]

In administrative work it has been noticeable that active attempts at interference in the internal administration of Cooch Behar by the British Government of Bengal began thereafter. Henry Douglas was appointed Resident Commissioner at Cooch Behar sometimes in 1789. What instructions he had from the Government are not known.[4] He applied himself mainly to regularize the Revenue administration. Dauglas was succeeded by Charles Andrew Bruse in 1791 and the latter by W. Towers Smith in 1795 who made over charge to Richard Ahmuty in 1797.[5] Francis Jenkins writing in 1849 states that he did not find on record anything to show what degree of control was to be exercised over Cooch Behar except as regards the right of minting money by the Maharaja. Specially during the rule of Maharaja Harendra Narayan came of age in 1801 and the office of the Resident Commissioner of Cooch Behar was terminated.[6]

In the meantime administrative reforms had been carried out in the Dewani districts of Bengal by Lord Cornwallis and the Cornwallis Code had been promulgated. In January 1803 the post of the Commissioner of Cooch Behar was revived and Francis Pierard was appointed Commissioner of Cooch Behar for the purpose of carrying into effect in the concert with the Maharaja, certain necessary arrangements for the collection of the public revenue and the administration of justice and for the adoption of a proper and efficient system of police.[7]

In early 1880's i.e during the period of nine years from 1805 to 1813 the Collector of Rangpur carried on the duties in connection with Cooch Behar from Rangpur.[8] The Collectors seem to have lent their ears to many a complaint against Maharaja Harendra Narayan and sent reports to the Council at Calcutta.[9] In such state of affairs the Government of Lord Minto recorded its Resolution in the Revenue Department dated August 7, 1813 and determined upon exercising a through and efficient interference into the internal affairs of Cooch Behar with a view to eradicating the evils of the administration. With this object in view the Government revived the office of the Commissioner of Cooch Behar and appointed Norman MacLeod to the post.[10]

As official records provided an important point that MacLeod failed in his task and was recalled shortly after and thus ended the attempts of the East India Company to interference in the affairs of Cooch Behar in their own way.[11]

The contact with the British Commissioners were not entirely devoid of result. While there was only one irregular court in 1788 and no arrangement for policing the State, in 1849 when Francis Jenkins, Agent of the Governor General inspected Cooch Behar he found the following regular courts presided over by officers specially appointed:[12]

A. Criminal Courts :

1. Two Criminal Courts of first instance, the court of the Foujdari Ahilkar and the Court of the Naib Ahilkar.
2. Court of Criminal Appeals and Court of Sessions presided over by a brother of the Maharaja.

B. Civil Courts :

1. Court of the Civil Judge (Ahilkar)
2. Court of Sadar Amin.
3. Court of Civil Appeals.

C. Revenue Courts :

1. Court of the Dewan for Khalsa lands.
2. A separate court for the Khangi lands.

D. The Rajsabha was nominally presided by the Maharaja assisted by the Dewan. This was the final court in all criminal matters.

In 1849 there were seven police thanas and outposts under the Foujdari Ahilkar. These were located at (i) Sadar or Kotwali, (ii) Dinhata, (iii), Mekhliganj, (iv) Giladanga, (v) Bhavaniganj, (vi) Shamganj and (vii) Changrabandha.[13]

Colonel Jenkins reports that the quality of work at the courts was more or less satisfactory though there was complaints of corruption among the amlahs. The presiding officers of the courts were but poorly paid and so also were the amlahs.[14] The pay was not disbursed out of the revenue of the State but out of the fees, fines and forfeitures in those courts. The police, being under the establishment of the Faujdari Ahilkar were expected to be paid by him out of the earnings of his court and Jenkins observed that more often than not the earnings of the Court of the Foujdari Ahilkar was insufficient to cover the salaries of the presiding officers of the Courts and the amlahs and there was nothing left to pay the police.[15]

This state of affairs continued till 1864. The British Government decided to take over charge of the State during the minority of the King Nripendra Narayan and deputed Colonel J. C. Haughton, the Agent of the Governor – General in the North Eastern Frontier as Commissioner in charge of the administration.[16] The Commissioner was vested with full powers of the ruler of the State except with regard to certain specific points namely grants of lands, gratuities and pensions and the confirmation of capital sentence. These powers were reserved by the Government. H. Beveridge was appointed Deputy Commissioner and he assumed charge on 4 November 1864.[17]

The State of the administration is best described in the words of the first Deputy Commissioner Beveridge from the Annual Report for 1865 -67. " Before the appointment of a British Commissioner the government of Cooch Behar was in a deplorable condition........., It was in fact a mongrel Government, being a cross as it were between the Bhutia or the Koch idea of government and those which the Bengali amla supposed to be ours."[18]

> "There was no cohesion or real subordination in any part of the administration from the top to the bottom. Every officer did what was right in his eyes, and acknowledged no authority but that of the Rajah and his subordination even to him was in most cases only lip-service ...."[19]

> "Former Commissioners had brought it also to the level of the zilla administration of their days and at that point it had stuck."[20]

Communicating on the poor pay of the officers Beveridge states:[21] "while of course holding that expenditure should be reduced as much as possible I am of opinion that a greater increase in the expenditure of the State in Civil administration must be accepted as a necessary consequences of the appointment of a British Commissioner...... it is impossible that a British officer can administer Cooch Behar without an efficient staff of subordinates and these can only be procured by giving liberal salaries."

Apart from that subsequent reforms worked in the following manner. Formerly, each office collecting revenue incurred expenditures out of the collections and only transmitted the balance if any to the treasury or Majudat.[22] The direction was given that all collecting officers were to send their entire collections to the Treasury and draw their disbursements by bills. This ensured regular payment of all grades of the staff. As the Maharaja was a minor the Raj sabha court was abolished and the functions were transferred to the Commissioner's office. The composition of the sessions Court was retained but a retired Session Judge from Government service was appointed.[23] The Sessions Judge was given appellate power over the decisions of the Fouzdari Ahilkar. Two additional Naib Ahilkars were appointed to clear off the accumulated cases in the court of the Fouzdari Ahilkar. The Indian Penal code was introduced in 1866 and the Indian Evidence Act and the Code of Criminal Procedure were introduced in 1873 with consequent charges in the court and in the police procedure. The first sub –division was established at Tufangunj on 3rd March 1866 and the four other sub –divisions were created in 1872.[24] The power of the Fouzdari Ahilkar was enhanced to the infliction of imprisonment up to two years and a fine up to Rs. 200 in Narayani rupees and the Naib Ahilkars in charge of the sub divisions were given power of taking cognizance. The spirit of the Bengal Cattle Trespass Act (Act III of 1857) and of the Gambling Act (Act II of 1867) were ordered to be followed in the courts. Formerly, the Rajguns or kinsmen of the Maharaja were not amenable to the jurisdiction of the Criminal court. In 1871 the jurisdiction of the court of the Deputy Commissioner who now exercised the functions of the Sessions Court was extended to the Rajgans.[25]

On the matter of State police force was all along a weak point Cooch Behar administration. Not only was the number of police personnel extremely meager but their salaries were a mere pittance and that too were hardly ever regularly paid. The police force was recognized in 1876 - 77 and consisted of one superintendent of police, three inspectors, eight sub –inspectors, twenty-six head constables and two hundred and forty constables. The number of police stations were increased to five, viz;. kotwali, Tufangunj (afterwards Fulbari), Dinhata, Mathabhanga and Mekhligunj. The outposts were increased to seven.[26]

On 8th November 1883 Maharaja Nripendra Narayan assumed charge and on the following day he issued the Memorandum of Administration drawn up by the Commissioner of Jalpaiguri and Cooch Behar Division. A Council of State was established with the Maharaja as President and three members, namely, the Superintendent of the State; the Dewan and the head of the Department of Civil Justice as members.[27] The Superintendent of the State was head of the Department of General Administration, the Dewan was the Head of the Department of Revenue and the Judicial Officer was the Head of the Civil Justice. The Superintendent was to supervise, control and direct the administration of Criminal Justice and the Police, the military, jail, public works, education and Audit departments and was to be the Session Judge to hear the Criminal Appeals.[28] The Dewan was to be in charge of the Revenue department and responsible for all collections and supervision of all the proceedings in such matters. The judicial member was to hear all Civil appeals and revenue appeals of certain classes and supervise the administration of Civil justice and all final appeals to the Council.[29]

In August 1885 the Commissioner of the Jalpaiguri Division was appointed by the Government of India to be the Ex – officio Political Agent of Cooch Behar and the Superintendent of Cooch Behar was appointed justice of the peace.[30]

In December 1891 the remarkable Memorandum of Administration was modified to some extent. The judicial functions of the Council were transferred to a Court of two members of the Council, the Bench being constituted by the Maharaja excluding that member against whose decision the appeal lay. In case of difference between the two members constituting the Bench the matter was re-heard by the full Council with the Maharaja presiding.[31]

The Civil judge was appointed Session Judge in addition and the Dewan was made an additional Sessions Judge. The Session's power hitherto exercised by the Superintendent ceased. The power of the fouzdari Ahilkar was redefined and made to correspond to the powers of a District Magistrate of British districts.[32]

For the next fifty years that is till the merger of Cooch Behar State into West Bengal and its formation into a district the administrative pattern remained the same. The only change made was that the members of the Council were designated Ministers and their offices designated Secretariats.[33]

After the signing of the Agreement of accession on 28th August 1949, the Government of India issued an order entitled the Cooch Behar (Administration) Order 1949 and appointed a chief commissioner at the head of the administration in Cooch Behar. The Chief Commissioner was vested with all the powers which under the laws operating in Cooch Behar were exercised by the Maharajas.[34] All the laws in force in Cooch Behar or any part thereof immediately before 12 September 1949 continued to remain in force until repealed or amended by a competent legislature or authority. All judges, magistrates and other officers who immediately before this date were to continue to exercise then respective functions in the same manner and to the same extent as they were doing before this order, until other provision was made by the Chief Commissioner.[35] All taxes, duties, cases or fees which immediately before the commencement of the order, were being lawfully levied in Cooch Behar or any part thereof were to continue to be levied and applied to the same purpose, until other provision was made by a competent legislature or authority.

During the governance of the Chief Commissioner that is from 12 September to 31

December 1949 the administration in Cooch Behar remained the same as before. On 1st January 1950 Cooch Behar was merged into West Bengal by a notification issued by the Government of India on 31 December 1949 entitled the States' Merger (West Bengal) Order, 1949.[36] A Deputy Commissioner and Administrator of Cooch Behar was appointed by the Government of West Bengal and from 1 January 1950 Cooch Behar became a district of West Bengal. As Cooch Behar was a part of India and a part of West Bengal already on 26 January 1950, the date on which the Constitution of India was adopted, the Constitution applied to Cooch Behar from that very date.[37]

The administrative set up consisted of a Deputy Commissioner and an Additional Deputy Commissioner, one Senior Deputy Collector (who was the previous Fouzdari Ahilkar), one Naib Ahilkar in charge of the Sadar sub –division, one Naib Ahilkar each in charge of the treasury and the Khas Mahal departments, two Additional Naib Ahilkars for revenue work at Sadar and one Additional Naib Ahilkar for criminal case work of the Sadar Sub –division.[38] In each of the Sub –divisions of Dinhata and Mathabhanga, there was one Naib Ahilkar in charge of the subdivision and one Additional Naib Ahilkar. In the sub divisions of Tufangunj and Mekhligunj there was only one Naib Ahilkar in charge of the sub–division. Initially, the Subdivisional Officers acted as Munsifs and as Sub–Registrars also. Later, they were relieved of these duties and separate Sub–Registrars and Munsifs were appointed.[39]

The police administration remained as before. The force was under a Superintendent of Police with two Deputy Superintendents at headquarters. Each of the eight police stations, via; Cooch Behar (Kotwali), Tufangunj, Dinhata, Sitai, Sitalkuchi, Mathabhanga, Mekhligunj and Haldibari was in charge of a sub–Inspector of police. At Mathabhanga and Dinhata there was a Circle Inspector at each place.[40]

The head of the district administration is the Deputy Commissioner who is also appointed District magistrate under the Criminal procedure Code. He is a member of the Indian Administrative Services. He is assisted in his administration by two Additional Deputy commissioner is in charge of Estates Acquisition and land Reforms while the other assists the Deputy Commissioner in General Administration. One Deputy collector is in charge of the Office of the Deputy Commissioner while another Deputy Magistrate and Deputy Collector is in charge of the Sadar Subdivision assisted by one Deputy Magistrate and Deputy Collector and one Sub – Deputy Magistrate and sub–Deputy Collector.[41] One Deputy Collector is the Regional Assistant Director of Panchayet and Executive Officer of the Zilla Parishad while another Deputy Collector is the District Panchayet Officer. A Joint Magistrate is the Settlement Officer for Cooch Behar. Jalpaiguri – Malda Revisional Settlement assisted by a Deputy Collector who is Assistant Settlement Officer. One Deputy Collector is the General Manager of the north Bengal State Transport Corporation assisted by a sub – Deputy

Collector as Administrative and Personnel Officer. One sub–Deputy Collector is Special Officer for Scheduled Castes and Tribes Welfare. A temporary sub–Deputy Collector in the District Compensation Officer for Estates Acquisition. All these officers are stationed at Cooch Behar.[42]

At Dinhata a Deputy Collector and Deputy Magistrate is in charge of the sub division assisted by a Deputy Magistrate and a sub–Deputy Magistrate for General Administration.

At Mathabhanga a Deputy Magistrate is in charge of the subdivision assisted by two sub-Deputy Magistrates for General Administration. At Tufanganj a Deputy Magistrate and Deputy Collector is in charge of the subdivision assisted by a sub- Deputy Magistrate for General Administration. At Mekhligunj similarly a Deputy Magistrate and Deputy Collector is in charge of the subdivision assisted by a sub-Deputy Magistrate for General Administration. Recently, the cadres of Deputy Collectors and sub- Deputy Collectors have been merged for the whole of West Bengal.[43]

A Superintendent of Police is the head of the police administration in the district assisted by an Additional Superintendent of Police, both of whom are members of the Indian Police Service. There are two Deputy Superintendents of Police at headquarters, one looking after the police lines, barracks and discipline while the other assists the Superintendent of Police in his work.[44] At each of the sub–subdivisions there is an Inspector of Police. The number of Police Stations continuos to be eight as before. The personnel has been strengthened by adding one more Sub – Inspector at each police station. The number of constables has also been increased.[45]

There were eleven Community Development Blocks in the district. These are Cooch Behar I, Cooch Behar II, Dinhata I, Dinhata II, Sitai, Mathabhanga I, Mathabhanga II, Sitalkuchi, Tufangunj, Mekhligunj and Haldibari.[46] The Block Development Officer is generally a member of the West Bengal Junior Civil Service (merged with the senior service) or a member of the Subordinate Agricultural Service.[47] The other complement of staff were the Agricultural Extension Officer, the Social Education Officer, the Sub – Assistant Engineer, the Social Education Officer, the sub – assistant Engineer, the Panchayet Extension Officer, the Inspector of Cooperative Societies, Lady Social education Officer for women's programme's, Gram Sevika. The Gram Sevaks are stationed in the rural areas, one for each Anchal Panchayret.[48]

Thus the system of administration in the state of Cooch Behar represents an unique system of modern India. From Colonial to new ages thus a systematic way has been visible in this kingdom, which reflects the modern means of administration in the monarchy.

NOTES AND REFERENCES

1. Majumdar Durgadas – W.B.D.G (Koch Bihar), 1977, p, 134.
2. *Ibid.*

3. *Ibid.*
4. *Ibid.*
5. *Loc. cit.*
6. *Ibid.*
7. *Ibid.*
8. *Ibid.*, p. 135.
9. *Ibid.*
10. *Loc.cit.*
11. *Ibid.*
12. *Ibid.*
13. *Ibid.*
14. *Ibid.*
15. *Ibid.*
16. *Ibid.*, p. 136.
17. *Ibid.*
18. *Ibid.*
19. *Ibid.*
20. *Ibid.*
21. *Ibid.*

    The low salaries may be illustrated: Ahilkar Rs. 100/-, Sheristadar Rs. 25/-, Peshkar Rs. 15/-, Treasurer Rs. 8/-, Treasury Officer Rs. 22.8/-; Superintendent of Public Works Rs. 18.12/-; Dharmadhyaksha or master of Religious ceremonies Rs. 7.8/-, Darogahs of thanas Rs. 10, Kotwal Rs. 8/-, Jamadar Rs. 4/-, Barkandazs Rs. 3/-

    All these in Narayani rupees which was about 60 per cent in value of the standard rupee.
22. *Ibid.*, p. 137.
23. *Ibid.*
24. *Loc.cit.*
25. *Loc.cit.*
26. *Ibid.*
27. *Ibid.*
28. *Ibid.*

29. *Ibid.*, p. 138.
30. *Ibid.*
31. *Loc.cit.*
32. *Ibid.*
33. *Ibid.*
34. *Ibid.*
35. *Ibid.*
36. *Ibid.*
37. *Ibid.*, p. 139.
38. *Loc.cit.*
39. *Ibid.*
40. *Ibid.*
41. *Ibid.*
42. *Loc.cit.*

    The Officers of the Cooch Behar State service had the designations of *Ahilkar*, *Naib Ahilkar* and Additional *Naib Ahilkar*. Till their final absorption in West Bengal cadres they retained their designations but worked as Deputy Collectors and sub–Deputy Collectors and those performing Magisterial work were vested with powers under the Criminal Procedure Code. Gradually, the posts of the sub–divisional officers were appointed from West Bengal State Civil Service.
43. *Ibid.*
44. *Ibid.*, p. 140.
45. *Ibid.*
46. *Ibid.*, p. 141.
47. *Ibid.*
48. *Loc.cit.*

1

Various Facets of Administration of the State

The State of Cooch Behar represented a royal history in every sphere of administrative units. As per records has concern in 1883 there were 8 criminal and 11 revenue and civil courts open. For police purpose, the State was divided into 6 *thanas* or police circles. In 1881–82, the regular police force numbered 300 officers and men. These figures shows 1 policeman to every 4.3 square miles of the area or to every 2,008 persons in the population.[1] The system of village watch had been gradually introduced and there were at the end of the 19th Century, 1,701 *Chaukidars*. In 1874, 2,674 criminal cases were instituted in which 2,614 persons were brought to trial of whom 1,748 or 66 per cent were convicted, showing 1 person convicted of an offence to every 304 of the population. Out of property to the value of 770 reported to be stolen, 209 or 27 per cent, was recovered.[2] There was one jail at Cooch Behar town. In 1874, the aggregate number of prisoners was 1,324 of whom 34 were to Rs. 478. The administration of Cooch Behar State was carried on by the Maharaja, assisted by a Council, consisting of three members, namely the Superintendent of the State was carried on by the Maharaja assisted by a Council, consisting of three members, namely, the Superintendent of the State, the *Dewan* or Chief Revenue Officer and the Civil Judge.[3] The Maharaja was the President of t he Council and in his absence the Superintendent of the State acted as Vice–President. The Superintendent of the State supervised directed and controlled the administration of criminal justice and the police, military, jail, public works, education and audit departments. He was also the Sessions Judge, hearing all criminal all criminal appeals which ordinarily lay to Session Judges in British districts.[4]

The people of Cooch Behar are generally peace– loving. In Table A is given the figures of cognizable and non–cognizable offences reported for selected years from 1876–77 to 1959. It will be seen that though from 1876 to 1959 the population had more than doubled itself there has been no appreciable increase in the number of cognizable offences.[5] The number of non–cognizable offences also remained almost the same till 1952. After 1952 the number of non–cognizable offences had increased. This is partly due to introduction of several laws which were not in force in the erstwhile State of Cooch Behar and partly due to improvement in communications which enabled the people to approach the courts with comparative ease.[6] Also offences of petty and trivial nature which were previously settled in the villages found their way to the courts. As regards cognizable offences the number was 1,644 in 1876-77. The lowest figure was 1,350 in 1923 -24. The highest figure was 2,214 in 1950.[7]

The next group of high figures were 1,704 in 1927 -28, 1,730 in 1928 -29 and 1,794 in 1929 – 30 and also 1,834 in 1951. The high figures from 1927 to 1930 were due to the new settlement of land, revenue and rent brought about at the time. This is common in all places when people having real or imagined grievances against the decisions of the Settlement Officers have recourse to paddy cutting theft cases as a preliminary to further litigation.[8] The high figures of 1950 and 1951 were due to the large scale migration of population across the Indo – east Pakistan border at this time and a general unsettled condition of the country. Barring these years the number of crime, both cognizable and non –cognizable, have remained almost constant for over 80 years.[9] The following table shows a graphic picture of such things:[10]

Table — A

Criminal Offences reported

Year	*Number of cognizable offences*	*Number of non– cognizable offences*	*Total*
1876 77	1,644	1,465	3,109
1901 – 02	1,366	1,182	2,548
1902 – 03	1,481	1,306	2,787
1903 – 04	1,490	1,474	2,964
1904 – 05	1,609	1,517	3,126

1921 – 22	1,530	1,110	2,640
1922 – 23	1,446	1,106	2,552
1923 – 24	1,350	1,018	2,368
1927 – 28	1,704	1,136	2,840
1928 – 29	1,730	1,172	1,902
1929 – 30	1,794	1,180	2,974
1933 – 34	1,454	841	2,974
1934 – 35	1,494	835	2,329
1950	2,274	1,024	3,298
1951	1,834	897	2,731
1952	1,658	1,220	2,887
1957	1,327	2,566	3,893
1959	1,576	3,156	4,732

Though the people are generally peaceful, certain heinous crime like dacoity, robbery, murder and culpable homicide did occur in this district from olden times. Most of the murders had their origin in domestic intrigue or connubial infidelity and were hardly ever for gain. Lives were rarely lost in disputes over land or other property in this district. The Deputy Commissioner of Cooch Behar in the Annual Administration Report of 1872–73 writes:[11] " The population is not much tempted to crime by want. In some places tigers and in this respect act more efficiently than any Chaukidar. On the other hand the absence of Zamindars, who settle many petty cases in the Zillas .... tend to increase the number of criminal cases brought to light."

The earliest record available of dacoities in any one year is for 1865 – 66, when there were

12 dacoities. In 1867–68 there were 16 and in the following year 14. In 1869–70 there were seven cases of dacoity and in 1870–71 five cases. In the famine year 1874–75 the number was 11 which seems to indicate that the people in general were not moved to crime by want.[12] The peculiar geographical situation of Cooch Behar makes the district a convenient place for the offence of dacoity. It has been stated there were enclaves within Cooch Behar which belonged to the district of Rangpur and that there were also enclaves of Cooch Behar within the districts of Rangpur and Jalpaiguri. It was thus easy for dacoits of Rangpur and Jalpaiguri to commit offences in Cooch Behar and escape into these enclaves and avoid quick apprehension. Similarly, these enclaves afforded easy shelter for persons of Cooch Behar who after committing the crime could escape to these enclaves. Actually during the Sanyasi disturbances the enclaves of Cooch Behar in Rungpur district and the Baikunthapur territory of the Raikats offered them shelter and became their dens.[13] The principal reason for the Government of the East India Company to attempt reorganization of the Police and the Criminal Courts in Cooch Behar during the reign of Harendra Narayan was to prevent the offences of dacoity being committed by stray bands of the Sanyasis still at large within the district of Rangpur. Another offence which was rather common was the offences of dacoity being committed by stray bands of the Sanyasis still at large within the district of Rangpur.[14] Another offence which was rather common was the offence of kidnapping. In most

of the cases this related to a ran-away wife. This was so frequent in early days that the Cooch Behar State Government enacted a special law to empower the Fouzdari Ahilkar to adopt a summary procedure for the apprehension of the run–away wife and her paramour and restoration of the wife to the husband.[15]

Heinous crimes are, however, increasing since 1951. In 1951 there were 117 dacoities. This probably was due to the disturbed condition of the district due to large migrations across the border. The number fell to 47 in 1952, 27 in 1953 and 20 in 1969. In 1970 and 1971 the number of dacoities increased to 113 and 114 respectively.[16] The number of murders were 6 in 1951, 11 in both the years 1952 and 1953, but it rose to 18 in 1969, 26 in 1970 and 34 in 1971. The number of rioting were 67 in 1951, 84 and 74 in 1952 and 1953, but it rose to 453 in 1969 and to 583 in 1970. There was slight diminution in the number of rioting in 1971 which was 327 that year. These increases tend to show that the one–time primitive peace–loving community of Cooch Behar was gradually changing its character.[17]

The history of the development in the police force has been describe in the following lines. The allround strength of regular police in the state of Cooch Behar was as follows. The State police force was under a Superintendent of Police assisted by one Addidtional Superintendent and two Deputy Superintendents. There were two Police Circles each under one Inspector, one located at Cooch Behar and the other at Mathabhanga. In addition, there was one Inspector for Cooch Behar Court and one each for the State Intelligence Branch. The State Enforcement Branch and Armed Police. The following table gives the distribution of the sub–Inspectors, Assistant Sub–inspectors, Head constables, constables, Dafadars and Chaukidars:[18]

Table -2

	S.I.	A.S.I.	H.C.	NAIK	CONS-TABLES	DAFA-DARS	CHAUKI-DARS
Cooch Behar	7	6	4		68		304
Tufangunj	3	3			14		216
Dinhata	4	3			14	28	258
Sitai	2	1			08	05	70
Mathabhanga	4	4			14		306
Sitalkuchi	2	1			10		130
Mekhligunj	2	2			10		82
Haldibari	2	1			10		71
Court	6	7	1		28		
D.I.B.	3	6			24		
D.E.B.	4	1			13		
Reserve	4				53		
Armed Police	3		30	49	348		
Miscellaneous	4	25			22		

Anti–corruption work in West Bengal is under a centralized organization under the vigilance commissioner. There was no prohibition in the State.[19]

There was a lock up (jail) at Cooch Behar and four sub-jails of Tufangunj, Dinhata, Mathabhnaga and Makhligunj. The Cooch Behar

State jail was under a whole time Superintendent, while the sub–jail were under the Sub–divisional Officers who act as ex-officio Superintendents of the sub–jails. The sub–jails were merely judicial lock–ups and no sentence in excess of one month's imprisonment was executed in the sub–jails. Recreational facilities such as cinema shows, sports and musical and yatra performances were arranged.[20] There was a Board of unofficial visitors for the district and the sub–jails.

Juvenile delinquents and political prisoners were not generally kept in the Cooch Behar jail but transferred elsewhere.[21]

The crafts taught in the Cooch Behar jail include carpentry making of jute twines, weaving, mat-making and works in bamboo.

A history of evolution of the Criminal and Civil courts in Cooch Behar has been formed since modern ages. Since 1950, that was after the merger of Cooch Behar with West Bengal the following Criminal Courts were functioning in the State:[22]

a) Sadar Sub divisional Magistrate's Court with two subordinate courts.

b) Court of Sub – divisional Magistrate of Tufangunj.

c) Court of the Sub- divisional Magistrate of Mathabhanga.

d) Court of Sub –divisional Magistrate of Dinhata.

e) Court of the Sub-divisional Magistrate of Mekhligunj.

There was a Civil and Sessions Judge at Cooch Behar in 1950 and the Sub-divisional Officers acted as Munsifs in addition to being Magistrates. From January 16, 1950 a State and Sessions Judge from West Bengal Cadre was posted at Cooch Behar. The following Courts were setup from 1951:[23]

1) One temporary Court of a Subordinate Judge for the district stationed at Cooch Behar.
2) One permanent *Munsif's* Court at Cooch Behar to be presided over by the Subordinate Judge.
3) One temporary *Munsif's* Court at Tufangunj to be presided over by the Subordinate Judge on circuit.
4) One permanent *Munsif's* Court at Mathabhanga with a Munsif stationed there.
5) One permanent *Munsif's* Court at Mekhligunj to be presided over by the *Munsif* of Mathabhanga on circuit.
6) One permanent *Munsif's* Court at Dinhata to be presided over by the *Munsif* of Mathabhanga on circuit.

The Sadar Judge, who was also the Sessions Judge for the district, functions as the Tribunal for the purpose of section 41 of the West Bengal Estate Acquisition Act and as special judge for the purpose of sections 5A and 20 of the said Act in Addition to his usual duties as District Judge.[24] He was also the Competent Authority for the purpose of Rehabilitation of Displaced

Persons and Eviction of Persons in Unauthorized Occupation of Land Act and the Authority under section 20 of the Minimum wages Act in respect of the district for the purpose of hearing and deciding claims under the Act.[25]

The Subordinate Judge was also the Assistant Sessions Judge of the State and exercises Small Cause Court powers up to the value of Rs. 750 within the local limits of the Sadar and Tufangunj, *Munsifs* and functions as an Appellate Authority under section 19(1) of the West Bengal Land Reforms Act, 1955, within the limits of the said two Munsifs in addition to his usual duties as Subordinate Judge.[26]

The *Munsif* of Mathabhanga who also presides over the Courts at Dinhata and Mekhligunj wa not vested with small Cause Court powers. He functions as an Appellate Authority under section 19 (1) of the West Bengal Land Reforms Act, 1955 within the limits of the said three *Munsifs* in addition to his duties as Munsifs.[27]

The Sessions Judge of Cooch Behar also presides over the Special Court of Cooch Behar created under the West Bengal Criminal Amendment (Special Court) Act, 1949. The Sessions Judge hears appeals, revision cases, motions, Criminal Miscellaneous cases arising out of orders and decisions of the Magistrates in the State. The Assistant Sessions Judge hears the appeals of persons convicted on trial by second and third Class Magistrate.[28]

The cases handled in the court of the District Judge were Original Suits, viz; Title Suits including contested Letters of Administration cases, Matrimonial Suits and their execution cases, Guardianship cases, Miscellaneous Judicial cases, Miscellaneous Non-Judicial cases, Title Appeals, Money Appeals, Rent Appeals, Miscllaneous Appeals and Special Miscellaneous Appeals.[29]

The cases handled in the Court of the Subordinate Judge are Original Suits, viz; Title Suits, Matrimonial Suits, Money Suits and Rent Suits of value exceeding Rs. 2,000, Small Cause Court Suits of value up to Rs. 750 in respect of the Sadar *Munsif* and their execution cases, Miscellaneous Judicial cases arising out of these suits and cases, Title Appeals, Rent Appeals, Money Appeals and Miscellaneous Appeals arising out of the decisions of the *Munsif* except where he himself acts as the Munsif in which case the Appeals were heard by the Sadar Judge.[30]

The cases handled in the Court of the Munsif were Original Suits, viz; Title Suits, Matrimonial Suits, Money Suits, Rent Suits up to the value of Rs. 2,000 and their execution cases, Miscellaneous Judicial cases arising out of these suits and cases and appeals under section 19(1) of the West Bengal Land Reforms Act, 1955.[31]

The work of the Panchayeti Adalat has not yet started in the State.

Previous to the Merger of Cooch Behar with West Bengal there were no Mukhtears as the Cooch Behar State Government did not allow Mukhtears to practice in the Court. After the Merger some Mukhtears have been enrolled. There was a Bar Association of the Pleaders at Cooch

Behar, Dinhata, Tufangunj, Mathabhanga and Mekhligunj.[32]

Petitioners adjudged as Paupers were allowed to file suits without the prepayment of Court Fees (other than fees payable for the service of processes). Undefended persons charged with murder were defended at State cost. Thus various facets were maintained during the rule of monarchy in the State.

NOTES AND REFERENCES

1. Majumdar Durgadas – *W.B.D.G(Koch Bihar),* 1977, p. 155.
2. *Ibid.*
3. *Loc.cit.*
4. *Ibid.*
5. *Ibid.*
6. *Ibid.*
7. *Ibid.*

   W.W.Hunter – *The Imperial Gazatteer of India,* Vol, VIII, Karens to Madnagarh, Second Edition, London, 1886, pp. 325-27.
8. *Ibid.*, p. 156.
9. *Ibid.*
10. *Loc.cit.*

    Figures from 1951 onward were taken from West Bengal District Census Handbook, 1961, Cooch Behar, 1966, p. 320.
11. *Ibid.*, p. 157.
12. *Ibid.*
13. *Ibid.*
14. *Ibid.*
15. *Ibid.*

16. *Loc.cit.*
17. *Ibid.*, p. 158.
18. *Loc.cit.*
19. *Ibid.*
20. *Ibid.*
21. *Ibid.*, p. 159.
22. *Ibid.*
23. *Ibid.*
24. *Ibid.*
25. *Loc.cit.*, p. 160.
26. *Ibid.*
27. *Ibid.*
28. *Ibid.*
29. *Ibid.*
30. *Ibid.*
31. *Ibid.*
32. *Ibid.*, p. 161.

2

A Force an Excellent Wing in the History of the State

The State of Cooch Behar gained a momentum during the rule of Maharajas. The well developed system has been introduced in every corner of the empire. The law and order system is not an exception to that. During the Rule of Maharaja an uniform system has been introduced in the State force which may be summarizes in the following way.

The following table given below shows the strength and cost of the Police during the post–official year:[1]

Strength		*Cost Rs.*
1	Superintendent	5,454/-
3	Inspectors	4,500/-
9	Sub – Inspectors	6,480/-
28	Head – Constables	5,280/-
259	Constables	20,436/-
	Total	42,150/-

The increase under the item of Superintendent's pay was due to the increments of Rs. 50 to his salary sanctioned two years ago viz., an increase of Rs. 100 in two annual increments of Rs. 50 each. The increase under the head of Sub–Inspectors was due to the appointment of an extra Sub–Inspector for Haldibari Police Station, which has been made a thana in consequence of its increased importance as a railway station on the principal road of the State.[2]

The Sub–Inspector was appointed last year, but was paid from savings, no provision having been made on the budget for the purpose. The increase in the number of constables and consequent increased cost was due to the appointment of 15 extra constables as guards for the sub–divisional lock–ups.[3]

Formerly the Sub–divisional treasure chest, which was kept in the guard house attached to the lock–up and the lock–up itself were under the guard of one sentry only. This man naturally kept watch near the door of the guard house where the treasure was kept. The far side of the lock–up was thus quite unguarded and on stormy nights it was easy for the prisoners, if they could get out of the bamboo house, to cross the palisade and escape without attracting any notice.[4] Two years ago it was the custom to keep a certain number of prisoners undergoing sentences of as much as six months at the lock–ups for local labour. At the Mathabhanga lock–up one of the doors which were made of wooden bars on a wooden framework, fastened with one padlock and chain half way from the ground to the top of the door, had got somewhat warped and the prisoners found that they could prize it open at the bottom, without breaking the chain, sufficiently to admit of a man forcing his way through.[5] This was actually done, for a short time, systematically and on dark rainy nights certain prisoners used to get out of the lock–up, go and commit thefts in the neighbourhood, dispose of their booty to accomplices outside and then return and lock themselves up.[6]

Thefts were reported to which no clue could be obtained and the real delinquents might have escaped detection and served out their time in jail, committing thefts by night with impunity, had it not been for the discovery of some tobacco in the lock–up in possession of a prisoner, who, when, about to be punished, informed against his comrades rather than suffer alone and so the whole thing came out.[7] The prisoners who had broken out confessed everything. They had preferred returning to prison each night that they had got out, to remaining at large with warrants perpetually hanging over them.[8]

The story reflects small credit on any of the parties concerned, but it was difficult to find fault, as the system was most to blame. One head constable and four constables were quite an inefficient guard for a lock–up and station house with a treasure chest in it, outside the lock–up in closure.[9] The guard has been doubled, the doors of the buildings inside the lock–up secured with double locks above and below and the sub–divisional officers prohibited from keeping prisoners sentenced to more than one weeks rigorous imprisonment in the lock–up.[10]

Working of the State Police force summarized as follows :[11]

Details	1877–78	1878–79
Cognizable cases reported including those pending Police enquiry at the end of the previous year	1,586	1,577
A Forms (true)	371	368
A Forms (false)	0	1
B Forms(true)	23	35
B Forms (false)	10	5
C Forms (true)	320	387
C Forms(false)	154	200
Cases not enquired into under sec.117 Code of Criminal Procedure	278	169
Cases taken up direct by Magistrate	362	396
Pending before the Police at the close	68	16

It will be observed that a number of A forms has decreased by 3. There was a decrease of 9 in the number of cases reported. The number of false cases, 206 against 164 of the previous year, shows an increase of 42 cases.[12] Besides the false cases mentioned above, 82 cases were found to be false amongst those that were taken up direct by the Magistrates. The total number of false cases were therefore, 288 or 20 percent of the total number of cognizable cases reported. 30 complainants were prosecuted under the sections 182 and 211 for lodging false complaints, of whom 19 were convicted and 11 released.[13] This was considered eminently satisfactory, knowing the difficulty of obtaining legal proof of the fact that a charge was false, however morally convinced as to its falsity one may be. Cases moreover were shown as false in the statements which were thrown out as being properly cognizable by the Civil Courts, although the charges made may have their foundations in fact and such cases go to diminish the proportion of convictions under sections 182 and 211, to the total number of charges shown as false in the statements.[14]

During the year under report one Sub–Inspector, five head constables and 25 constables were punished for various offences under the Penal Code. There were no cases of extortion of confession by torture, or cruelty against any of the Police. The *Fouzdari Ahilkar* however notices that cases of oppression by *Chowkidars* have came to his notice in which he has little doubt that the *Chowkidars* were only the tools of the regular Police.[15] Exceptional punishment has been dealt out in such cases and when the *Chowkidars* come to understand their position better and learn their duties and such complaints will be of rare occurrence. They arise out of an exaggerated idea entertained by the *Chowkidar* of the Power of the regular policeman over him personally.[16]

In last year record it has been mentioned that a force of 870 *Chowkidars* had sprung up spontaneously and that the number was rapidly increasing. Out of 930 *talooks* in the State 829 have got 1,534 *Chowkidars* and 101 still remain without *Chowkidars*. Petitions for the appointment of *Chowkidars* were still came in. Hitherto the State has spent nothing on this new auxiliary Police force, but the following year the sanction to supply the men with badges and spear heads as insignia of office. It would be advisable also to adopt the rules in force in the neighboring districts of Rungpore and Jalpaiguri regarding *Chowkidars* for the better control of this large body of men.[17]

As before stated these *Chowkidars* were paid by voluntary contributions with s view to enforcing the continuance of such payments without at the same time alarming the people with the idea of a new tax had called for a report as to the distribution and incidence of the gross payments preparatory to recommending that rules be passed to enable to realize from defaulters their quota of subscription and to fix the proportions in which the different grades of tenants shall pay according to the size of their holdings &c. in the future.[18]

The following two tables will show the percentage of acquittals to convictions in cognizable cases taken up direct by Magistrates and in cases sent up by the Police separately.

Result of trial of persons in Cognizable cases including those taken up direct by Magistrate:[19]

Total number of persons in Columns XV of Cognizable return	Acquitted &c., Columns XVI and XVII	Convicted &c., Columns XVIII A and B	Pending &c., Columns XIX, XXII, XIII	Percentage of Conviction
912	256	601	15	67

Result of trial of persons in Cognizable cases investigated by Police :[20]

Persons sent up for trial including those pending from last year	Acquitted &c.	Convicted	Pending and died.	Percentage of conviction
578	138	423	12	75.6

These results are creditable to the Police.

The percentage of property recovered to property stolen is only a fraction better than last year as shown in the annexed table.

Abstract Statement of property stolen and recovered :[21]

1877 - 78			1878 - 79		
Amount of property stolen	Amount of property recovered	Percentage of recovery	Amount of property stolen	Amount of property recovered	Percentage of recovery
Rs. As. P. 12,055 0 0	Rs. As. P. 2,083 0 0	17.27	Rs. As. P. 15,181 0 0	Rs. As. P. 2,854 0 0	18.79

It is true that the nature of the State in Cooch Behar offers exceptional advantages for concealment. But what Superintendent consider unsatisfactory is that so many confessions result in so small a recovery of property admitted to have been stolen.[22]

Of 38 persons brought to trial for bad livelihood during the year 27 were ordered to find security.

The following table shows the fluctuations during the past five years in some of the principal classes of offences.[23]

CRIME	1874 – 75	1875 – 76	1876 – 77	1877 – 78	1878 – 79	REMARKS
Dacoity	11	6	1	2	3	Cases of theft in a building were previous to 1875 wrongly entered apparently as lurking house trespass.
Robbery	3	3	3	2	1	
Ordinary theft	397	727	746	838	736	
Lurking House trespass	314	34	13	5	8	
Murder	3	2	1	4	2	
Culpable Homicide	---------	2	5	1	6	

There were six escapes from police custody during the year. 4 of the prisoners escaping were recaptured.

The following officers are mentioned as especially deserving of commendation for detective ability:[24]

Sub–Inspector Guru Prosanna Singha

Sub–Inspector Momtazuddin

Sub-inspector Mohammad Johar

Head Constable Nazeeruddin

Sub–Inspector Sham Lall Mookerjee who was dismissed two years ago whose senior Inspector for permitting a case of extortion of confession in his immediate vicinity, but subsequently readmitted on account of previous long and good service, has throughout the year rendered himself very useful at Huldibari and performed his duties creditably.[25]

Inspector Parbutty Charan Chuckerbutty also deserves favourable mention as an officer of intelligence and ability. Babu Satya Charn

Mookerjea the Superintendent of police continuous to discharge the duties of his post satisfactorily.[26]

In 1880 The following table shows the strength of the Force together with the cost during the past official year :[27]

Designation	Cost Rs.
1 Superintendent of Police	5,454
3 Inspector	4,500
9 Sub – Inspector	6,480
28 Head – Constables	5,280
259 Constables	20,436
Total	42,150

The numbers and amount are exactly the same as for previous year.

The working of the Police was shown in the following table :[28]

Details	1879–80	1880–81
Cognizable cases reported including those pending Police enquiry at the end of the previous year	1,255	1,048
A. Forms (true)	258	234
B. Forms (true)	18	12
C. Forms (false)	8	9
C. Forms (true)	312	224
C. Forms (false)	127	89
Cases not enquired into under Section 117, C. P. Code	194	169
Cases taken up direct by Magistrates	326	302
Pending enquiry at the close of the year	12	9
Total	1,255	1,048

The number of A Forms was 234 against 258 of the preceding year, showing a decrease of 24;

but considering that the total number of cases instituted directly before the Police was 746 against 929 or 183 causes less than those in the previous year, the result was satisfactory. The number of false cases has also come down from 135 to 98 only. Eleven men were prosecuted for instituting false cases; of these nine were convicted and two released. These prosecutions, probably had much to do with the reduction of false complaints.[29]

The result of trial of persons in cognizable cases investigated by Police *suo motu* as compared with those of the previous year:[30]

YEAR	Persons sent up for trial including those from the last year	Acquitted	Convicted	Pending, died &c.	Percentage of convictions
1879 – 80	434	95	311	28	76.6
1880 – 81	432	106	310	16	74.5

The percentage of convictions in Police cases was 74.5 against 76.6 of the previous year. Though there was a slight decrease still the result was satisfactory when compared with similar figures in government Districts. The percentage in cognizable cases was 69.6 against 61.3 of the previous year. There was therefore an improvement of 8.3 which was very satisfactory.[31]

Conduct of the police : Four head–constables and eight constables were judicially punished during the year under report against two head–constables and 15 constables in the previous year.

The result compares favourably with previous year, as the number of constables punished has fallen from 15 to 7 a very small number out of a total of 259.[32]

The under mentioned officers are specially well spoken of by the *Fouzdari Ahilkar* and the Superintendent of Police :[33]

Sub–Inspector, Gooru Prosonno Singh

Officiating Sub–Inspector, Basseruddin

Head–constable, Naziruddin.

Village *Chowkidars*: The number of *Chowkidars*, at the end of the previous year was 1,554. Applications were received from the residents of five *Talooks* during the year under report and five men were appointed with the sanction of the authorities. Thus the total number of *Chowkidars* in the Raj was 1,559. A proposal for the introduction of the Government *Chowkidary* Act into this Raj was under consideration. Predecessor's opinion was and concur with in it, that any legislation in this direction must be very gradually and carefully undertaken if ultimate success was to be ensured.[34]

The sub – joined table shows the amount of property stolen and recovered during the year as compared with that of previous year :[35]

1879 - 80			1880 - 81		
Amount of property stolen	Amount of property recovered	Percentage of recovery	Amount of property stolen	Amount of property recovered	Percentage of recovery
Rs. A. P. 3,751 0 0	Rs. A. P. 2,340 0 0	26.7	Rs. A. P. 10,490 0 0	Rs. A. P. 2,287 0 0	21.8

The result was not at all satisfactory. The percentage in the last year was 26.7. This falling off is explained by the Superintendent by the fact that the stolen property was chiefly cash which the Police were unsuccessful in recovering.[36]

The general conduct of the Force has been good. There were only four escapes from custody against nine in the previous year. All of these persons were recaptured.

The Superintendent of Police was not in charge during the entire year. During his absence Babu Satinath Banerjee was in charge during the entire year. During his absence Babu Jadub Chander Chuckerbutty, Fauzdari Ahilkar, Babu Satya Charan Mookcrjcc rcvcrtcd to his own appointment on 16th Mookerjee is a painstaking and careful officer, but I shall of course be better able to give an opinion regarding him when I have had personal experience of his work during the current year.[37]

Under orders of Government contained in letter No.377 of 23rd February 1881, Mr. H.N.Harris, District Superintendent of Police of Rungpore, was specially deputed to inspect and report upon the working of the Police in Cooch Behar. This officer visited all the Police stations and made a careful inspection of the office of the Superintendent and submitted an exhaustive report in which he made a great many suggestions for the general improvement of the Police in the State. The chief points noted by him were as follows:[38]

a) That some special rules should be drawn up for keeping all books, registers, files &c., especially the Registers of convicts (which is complete) and absconded prisoners. That the mode of keeping accounts, cash, &c. are faulty and should be remodeled in the Bengal system.

b) That new accoutrements are required of the Regulation pattern.

c) That the Inspectors and Sub–Inspectors are as intelligent a body as ant in Bengal and the men appeared to be a fine well set up lot of up country men and that local recruiting should be encouraged as much as possible.

d) That a Sub Inspector on Rs. 60 should not be wasted upon drilling duty only. A man on Rs. 25 could be found perfectly competent for his duty.

e) That promotion has been fairly and equally distributed.

f) That there should be a half yearly inspection by the Superintendent of all the offices, Police stations and out-posts under his charge and that the results of this inspection should be recorded in writing with the remarks of the inspecting officer.

g) That instead of three Inspectors one would be sufficient for Cooch Behar.

h) That the proportion of cases not enquired into under Section 117 of the Procedure Code is too high

i) That there is very great delay in the submission of special reports from the office of the Superintendent of Police.

j) That although cases are taken up very promptly at the Police stations, the diaries are not sufficiently concise.

k) That the superintendent bore a very high character in the Rajshye and Pubna Police and that he has taken great pains with the Cooch Behar Force and that he is an intelligent and hard working officer but that a little more personal supervision over the conduct of enquires into cases should be exercised by him.

Prompt measures have been taken for the rectification of the regularities noticed by Mr. Harris.

Neither the Superintendent of the State's predecessor nor any one agree with Mr. Harris recommendations regarding the reduction of two inspectors.[39]

With reference to the issuing of new arms accoutrements that it would cost about Rs. 4,000 to substitute the carbine for the present weapon and such a large expenditure requires further consideration.[40] It was complained that the weapon at present used was too heavy for police work. This however, was a defect which was not of so much consequence in the case of a policeman as in that of a soldier.[41]

With regard to local recruiting for the Police instructed the Superintendent to carry out Mr.

Harris suggestion as far as he can do so consistently with considerations of efficiency.[42]

In all other points with Mr. Harris and his suggestions were being generally carried on.

With regard to Mr. Harris's remarks that the Superintendent should exercise a little more personal supervision over the enquiry into cases it was only fair to Babu Satya Charan Mookerjee to state that he was only in charge of the Police for 3 and half months out of the nine months work on which Mr. Harris's report was framed.[43]

The following table shows the strength and cost of the Force during the year :[44]

Designation	Annual cost
1. Superintendent	5,280 (a)
1. Assistant Superintendent	400 (b)
3. Inspectors	4,500
10 Sub–Inspectors	6,480
29 Head–Constables	5,580
265 Constables	24,228 (c)
Total	46,468

His Highness considered that the pay of the constables was too low and should be raised Rs. 1 all round.

The following Statement compares the working of the force for the past year with the preceding one, classifying the cases according to the prescribed forms:[45]

STATEMENT - A

Details	**1882–83**	**1883–84**
Cognizable cases reported including those pending Police enquiry at the end of the previous year	1,003	1,015
A Forms (true)	274	216
Ditto (false)	—	—
B Forms (true)	4	6
Ditto (false)	—	—
C. Forms (true)	269	349
Ditto (false)	104	117
Cases not required into under Section 157 C.P.Code	26	47
Cases taken up direct by the Magistrates	322	258
Pending enquiry at the close of the year	4	22

From the above statement, it appears that cognizable cases have increased by 12 and false cases by 13 during the year under report. The number of A forms has decreased by 58 and that of cases taken up direct by the Magistrate by 64. The increase in a number of cognizable cases was prescribed by the Superintendent to the following causes.[46]

"The promptness with which the village Policeman lays information at the Thana of every crime committed in his Mohallah.

2ndly; The lenient sentences with which habitual were punished by judicial officers in this State.

3rdly, The partial failure of the Bitri and Haimanti crops owing to scanty rainfall and the facilities offered by the Railway to the thieves from other districts who can come and got away from the State far more easily and quickly than in former times.

Information regarding details of crime cases and the results of prosecutions will be found under the heading " administration of Criminal Justice."[47]

The following comparative statement will show the number of cases reported as also the number of cases not required into, under section 157 Criminal Procedure Code with the percentage of cases not enquired into a cases reported for the past two year:[48]

No. of cases reported		No. of cases not enquired into		Percentage of cases not enquired into the cases reported		REMARKS
1882 – 83	1883 – 84	1882 – 83	1883 – 84	1882 – 83	1883 – 84	
1,003	1,015	25	47	2.5	4.6	There was an increase of 2.1 percent in the number of cases not enquired into under section 157 Criminal Procedure Code. The increase was attributable to the fact that in several petty thefts no investigation was made as the property stolen in them was not identifiable.

Statement of property stolen and recovered:[49]

1882 – 83			1883 – 84		
Amount of property stolen	Amount of property recovered	Percentage of recovery	Amount of property stolen	Amount of property recovered	Percentage of recovery
14,863	4,219	28.3	6,848	1,863	27.2

The percentage of property recovered was 27.2 during the year under report against 28.3 in the previous year which shows a slight falling off of 1.1 this needs no explanation.

Result of trial of persons in cognizable cases including those taken up direct by the Magistrate:[50]

YEAR	Total No. of persons in column XV of cognizable return	Acquitted &c., in column XVI, XVII and XIX	Convicted &c. in column XVIII a and b	Pending to columns XXII and XXIII	Percentage of convictions
1882 – 83	970	310	608	52	56.2
1883 – 84	790	264	513	12	65.9

Result of trial of persons in cognizable cases investigated by the Police: [51]

YEARS	Persons sent up for trial including those pending from the last year	Acquitted &c.	Convicted &c.	Pending and died &c.	Percentage of convictions
1882 – 83	494	123	337	34	73.26
1883 – 84	444	108	296	40	73.26

There were four cases of bad livelihood during the year under report against 12 in the preceding year, showing a decrease of 8.

In the above cases 4 persons were sent up for trial and in one case pending from last year, one person was awaiting trial. This makes a total of 5 persons all of whom were convicted during the year under review.

The Superintendent remarks as follows :[52]

> "There has been a falling off in the prosecutions for bad livelihood. This was owing to the breaking up of gangs of evils who have been convicted and sentenced to long term of imprisonment in dacoity cases during the last few years".
>
> "My experience was the same as that of Mr. Dalton, the late Deputy Commissioner, who in his report upon the year 1882 – 83, says in remarking on this subject.
>
> Most of the serious offences that have been detected in Cooch Behar since I have known it, have been the work of up – countrymen, who have come in gangs from Ghazipore and elsewhere."

The following table shows the fluctuations during the past 5 years in offences of a grave nature:[53]

Crimes	1879–80	1880–81	1881–82	1882–83	1883–84	REMARKS
Dacoity	--------	2	3	2	4	
Robbery	2	------	5	------	--------	
Murder	2	2	6	2	2	
Culpable homicide	2	2	1	------	1	

Equipment and discipline of the Force : During the year under report new accoutrements were procured and distributed amongst the men in the reserve as well as those in the Stations and Out–posts. The conduct of the Force was fair during the year under review.[54]

The number of escapes from Police custody was nil against one in the previous year. The result was creditable to the Police.

The Superintendent makes the following remarks regarding the *Chowkidary* system. "This institution, as it were, the backbone of a country and wherever measures have been adopted for bettering the position of the *Chowkidars* by ensuing regularity of payment of their wages, they have worked well and acted as a medium between the villagers and the Police in the way of rendering assistance in the investigation of cases. The want of an Act to ensure regularity of payment of their wages was greatly felt and sooner Act VI of 1870 with modifications adopted to this country was also introduced here, the better will they did their work."[55]

The introduction of an Act was under discussion. The number of *Chowkidars* was 1578 against 1576 in the previous year. There was no professional crime worth special notice reported during the year. Statement of accidental or unnatural deaths. This statement will speak for itself. There were 34 cases of snake- bits against 37 in the preceding year.[56]

During the year under report there were only 5 fairs in the Cooch Behar State. The first was at Gadadhar, the second was at Kalirghat in the Kotwali Station, the 3rd was at Haldibari, the 4th was at Sitalkuchi and the 5th at Sisubtalla. Two thefts occurred in the Haldibari fair. In these, property valued at Rs. 229 – 7 was stolen. The Police were not successful in these cases.[57]

The Superintendent of Police remained in charge of the office throughout the year with the exception of 22 days when he was absent on leave and 1st grade Inspector Parbati Charan Chakrabutty conducted the current duties of the office.[58]

Mr. C.E. Briscoe was appointed Assistant Superintendent of Police in December last. The Superintendent reports very well of this officer's energy and ability.

The number of cattle pounds was 40, the same as in the preceding year. The receipts for the year under report were Rs. 6,192 – 9 – 3 against Rs. 5,785 – 14 - 3 in the preceding year, showing an increase of Rs. 406 – 11. The disbursements were Rs. 2,914 – 6 – 0 against Rs. 3,422 – 9 – 9 in the previous year, showing a decrease of Rs. 508 – 3 – 9. The net profit therefore was Rs. 3,287 – 3 – 3 against Rs. 2,363 – 4 – 6. This shows an increase of Rs. 914 – 14 – 9.[59]

The Cattle Trespass Act was formally passed by His Highness the maharaja in Council on the 27th November 1883. Under the provisions of the Act, the posts of Pound *Mohurrirs* employed in all the Police posts were abolished and writer constables were entrusted with the work connected with the cattle Pounds. They draw a monthly allowance of Rs. 2 each in addition to their pay. The introduction of this Act has caused a saving of Rs. 144 in the cost of establishment.[60]

The dak establishment worked well during the year under report. Two more runners were appointed on the removal of the Tufangunj station to fulbari and Bhoishkhuchi out-post of Modhurbasha.

The following list will show the distances of stations and out–posts from Head – quarters together with the dates on which they were inspected by the superintendent of Police and the Inspector who was in charge of the office during the Superintendent of Police's absence on leave:[61]

Name of the Stations and out-posts	Distance r miles	April 1883	May 1883	June 1883	July 1883	August 1883	Sept. 1883	Oct 1883	Nov. 1883	Dec. 1883	Jan. 1884	Feb. 1884	March 1884
Kotwali Station	----	----	----	----	----	20	----	----	----	----	10	16	----
Toofangunj "	12	----	----	----	----	----	----	----	----	4	----	18	30
Dinhata "	14	----	----	----	----	----	30	----	----	27	4	22	18
Mathabhanga "	17	----	27	22	11	----	----	----	----	16	----	----	13
Mekhligunj "	25	----	----	10	----	----	----	----	----	16	----	----	3
Haldibari	43	----	----	17	----	----	----	----	----	17	----	----	7
Kholta Out post	12	----	----	----	14	----	13	----	----	9, 29	----	3	
Bhoshkoochi "	30	----	----	----	----	----	----	----	----	5	----	27	
Gitaldaha "	22	----	----	----	----	----	29	----	----	27	----	----	
Shitai	28	----	----	----	----	----	----	----	----	----	----	10, 23	
Shitalkuchi	29	----	----	----	----	----	----	----	----	----	----	24	
Kheti	33	----	----	----	----	----	----	----	----	----	----	25	
Kotebhari	51	____	----	15	----	----	----	----	____	8	----	----	

* The kotwali station was several times inspected by the Superintendent of Police during the year under report but the remarks regarding all inspections were not formally recorded.

From the foregoing table it would appear that the duty of inspection was carried on properly. The Superintendent of Police made two tours and thoroughly inspected every station and out-post. In the last tour the Assistant Superintendent of Police accompanied him and visited every Police post. This was done by special orders that Mr. Briscoe might become acquainted with every station and out–post in the State.[62]

The Superintendent of Police investigated 25 cases. 23 of these were cases of bribery against the Police and the remaining 2 were dacoit cases.

The Superintendent remarks as follows on the point :[63]

> "The subject of reconviction does not appear to have received proper attention. Annexed was a list of sentences passed which will show that habitual criminals have been inadequately punished. There can be no doubt that in awarding punishment unless habitual are treated with severity, diminution in crime cannot be expected and people will not enjoy freedom from the depredations of incorrigible offenders. In Government districts the procedure of punishing habitual offenders with severity has been thoroughly understood and wherever it has been adopted crime has decreased to a great extent. In Bengal there is a proverb which goes round every household "*badmash sashan nekmash palan*".

The *Fouzdari Ahilkar's* attention will be called to the subject and a report called for.

A list of men who have reconvicted during the year under review :[64]

SUB - DIVISIONS	Name of offenders	Crime	Sentence
Sudder Sub – division	Hagunu Nashya	380 I.P.C	After two previous convictions in cases under sections 380 and 411, I.P.C. was sentenced to 2 years rigorous imprisonment under Section 380, I.P.C. in the present case.
Ditto	Sridhar Dass	456 I.P.C	Convicted under section 380, I.P.C. and in the present case sentenced to 6 months rigorous imprisonment.
Ditto	Khetter Nashya	380 I.P.C	Twice convicted under section 379 and 380, I.P.C. and sentenced in the present case to 6 months rigorous imprisonment.
Dinhata Sub–divisions	Ali Mohamed	109 I.P.C	After two previous convictions in cases under section 457 and 380 I.P.C was sentenced in the present case to furnish a security for good behavior for 3 months only, in default to undergo rigorous imprisonment for the same period.
Ditto	Lalbar Nashya	414 I.P.C	Convicted once under section 380 and 411 I.P.C and sentenced in the present case to 6 months rigorous imprisonment.
Ditto	Hari Dass	457 I.P.C	Previous twice convicted under section 379 and 380 I.P.C. and sentenced to 6 months rigorous imprisonment in the present case.
Mathabhanga Sub - division	Matroo Dass	457 and 428 I.P.C	After two previous convictions under section 380 and 457 and 511 I.P.C was sentenced in the present case to pay a fine of Rs 7 in default to undergo rigorous imprisonment only.
Ditto	Shebar Nashya	457 I.P.C	Once before convicted under section 457 I.P.C. and sentenced in the present case to 6 months rigorous imprisonment only.
Ditto	Sadafor Dass	380 I.P.C	Once before convicted under section 457 I.P.C. and sentenced in the present case to one month's rigorous imprisonment.

During the year under review, 53 licenses were taken out against 51 in the previous year. As per regulation No. 3. And 91 old regulation No. 4. Of these 2 were quite unserviceable and 2 are under repairs.[65]

The following officers deserve special commendation for good service during the year:[66]

Inspector Parbati Charan Chakrabarti

Sub–Inspector Guru Prasanna Singha

Head Constable, Mahesh Chandra Raha.

The Superintendent of Police, Babu Satya Charan Mukherjee has shown zeal and ability in the charge of the Police department during the year.[67]

In 1885 the *Fouzdari Ahilkar* reports as follows:[68]

"One sub–Inspector, two Head–constables and 12 constables were judicially punished during the year under report against six Head–constables and 19 constables of the previous year. Sub–inspector Gurur Prasanna Singha and Head–constable Mokhtearuddin have done excellent service during the year under report. The former has already been rewarded by the Your Highness in Council by the grant of the Permanent increment of Rs. 10 to his pay; but the latter's services remain yet unrewarded. He was an old Officer of 17 years standing and successfully enquired into no less than 15 theft cases during the year. Several gangs of thieves in the neighbourhood of the sudder station were brought to justice by the Head –constables. The first vacancy in the post of a sub–inspector should be filled up by giving him a promotion which he so richly deserves. In my letter No. 441, dated the 4th December 1884, I had called the attention of the Superintendent of Police to the services of the Head–constable."

The charge of the Police office rested with the Superintendent of Police Babu Satya Charan Mukherjee from April 1884 to the 24th of February 1885, when he was appointed to act as Fouzdari Ahilkar. The Assistant Superintendent of Police during Babu Satya Charan Mukherjee's absence on deputation.[69]

Cognizable cases reported in 1883 – 84 1,015 and as per column IV and V of Statement A, Part I in 1884 – 85 1,233:[70]

STATEMENT - A

Details	1882–83	1883–84
Cognizable cases reported including those pending Police enquiry at the end of the previous year	1,015	1,233
A. Forms (true)	216	299
Ditto (false)	———	———
B. Forms (true)	6	3
Ditto (false)	———	———
C. Forms (true)	349	355
Ditto (false)	117	142
Cases not required into under Section 157 C.P. Code	47	52
Cases taken up direct by the Magistrates	258	367
Pending enquiry at the close of the year	22	15

From the above statement it would appear that during the year under report, cognizable cases have increased by 83 and that of cases taken up direct by the Magistrate by 109. This increase, which was chiefly observable in thefts, was due firstly to the partial failure of the crops which impelled poor people to commit petty thefts and secondly to the development of the *chowkidary* system under which the information of an offence can be more easily laid before the Police.[71]

During the year under review there were 3 cases of dacoit against 4 in the preceding year. In the 1st case which occurred at Boor Boori in Mathabhanga, 10 men were sent up for trial all of whom were discharged by the *Naib Ahilkar* of that sub–division for want of sufficient evidence. In the 2nd case which took place at Hoodoomdanga in Haldibari, 4 men were sent up for trial, but they were discharged for want of sufficient evidence by the *Naib Ahilkar* of Mekhligunj. The 3rd case happened at Dahola Khagrabari in Haldibari. In this 2 men were sent up but were awaiting trial before the *Naib Ahilkar* of Mekhligunj at the close of the year.[72]

There were 4 murders during the year under report against 2 in the preceding year, showing an increase of 2 cases. In the first case, which occurred at Brahmotra chatra in Dinhata 3 men were sent up for trial all of whom were convicted under Section 302 I.P.C. and sentenced to transportation for life. The 2nd case took place at Kajoldighi in Haldibari. The offender absconded immediately after committing the murder.[73] A reward of Rs. 50 has been offered for his apprehension. In the 3rd case, which occurred at Magoor mari in Kheti out–post, one person was sent up for trial but was discharged by the *Naib Ahilkar* of Mathabhanga for want of sufficient evidence. The 4th case happened at Pushnadanga in the Sudder Station. In this, one man was sent up for trial and sentenced to transportation for life by the Sessions Court under Section 302 I.P.C.[74]

During the year under review, there was only one case of culpable homicide as in the previous year. There were 398 cases of house – breaking and theft during the year under review against 391 in the preceding year. This shows an increase of 7 cases. During the year under report, there were only 12 cases of lurking house trespass against 16 in the previous year showing a decrease of 4 cases.[75]

During the year under review there were 22 cases of cattle theft against 18 in the preceding year showing an increase of four cases. During the year under report there were 12 cases of kidnapping against six in the preceding year showing an increase of six cases.[76]

During the year under review, 52 cases were not enquired into under Section 157, C.P.C. against 47 in the previous year.

The following comparative statement will show the number of cases reported as also the number of cases not enquired into under Section 157 C.P.C. with the percentage of cases not required into, to cases reported for the past two years.[77]

No. of cases reported		No. of cases not enquired into		Percentage of cases not enquired into the cases reported		REMARKS
1883 – 84	1884 – 85	1883 - 84	1884 – 85	1883 – 84	1884 – 85	
1015	1233	47	52	4.6	4.2	There is a decrease of 4 percent in the number of cases not enquired into under section 157 Criminal Procedure Code. The result is satisfactory.

Statement of property stolen and recovered:[78]

1883 - 84			1884 - 85		
Amount of property stolen	Amount of property recovered	Percentage of recovery	Amount of property stolen	Amount of property recovered	Percentage of recovery
6,848	1,863	27.2	8,933	3,540	39.9

During the year under report the percentage of property recovered was 39.6 against 27.2 in the preceding year showing an increase of 12.4. The improved result was satisfactory.[79]

The result of trial of persons in cognizable cases including those taken up direct by the Magistrate:[80]

YEARS	Persons sent up for trial including those pending from the last year	Acquitted &c.	Convicted &c.	Pending and died &c.	Percentage of convictions
1883 – 84	790	264	513	12	65.9
1884 – 85	1,054	373	580	101	60.8

The percentage of convictions has fallen off by 5.1. The result was bad. It was attributable to the change of magisterial officers and the consequent necessity of recording evidence in cognizable cases.[81]

During the year, 1884 under report there were 7 cases of bad livelihood against 4 in the previous year. This shows an increase of three cases. In 6 of these 6 men were sent up for trial. Five of whom were ordered to give security for good behavior, 1 being let off by the Magistrate. The remaining case was pending enquiry before the police at the close of the year.[82]

The following table shows the fluctuations during the past five years in offences which actually occurred in some of the principal classes:[83]

CRIMES	1880 – 81	1881 – 82	1882 – 83	1883 – 84	1884 – 85	REMARKS
Dacoit	2	3	2	4	3	
Robbery	--------	5	--------	----------	3	
Murder	2	6	2	2	4	
Culpable homicide	2	1	-------	1 (a)	1	

(a) This case was reported as murder but the Sessions Court decided it as culpable homicide. It was entered as murder by mistake in the last year's crime return statement A part I.[84]

The accoutrements were in good condition. The conduct of the force was good during the year under report.

During the year under review there were three escapes from Police custody against nil in the previous year.

The following table shows the strength of the Force together with the cost:[85]

	Designation	Annual cost.
1	Superintendent of Police	5,940 (a)
1	Assistant Superintendent of Police	1,200
3	Inspectors	4,500
10	Sub–Inspectors	6,480
30	Head constables	5,760 (b)
269	Constables	24,564 (c)
	Total	48,444

(a) The increase of Rs. 660 was due to the increase of pay at Rs. 55 per month

(b) The increase of Rs. 180 was due to the appointment of a 3rd grade head constable for Balarampore out–post.

(c) The increase of Rs. 336 was due to the appointment of 4 third grade constables for Balarampore out–post.

The Superintendent of Police makes the following remarks :[86]

> "The attention of the higher authorities has often been solicited to this important subject. The annexed list will show that habitual criminals have been inadequately punished. It was an undoubted fact that unless habitual were treated with severity, crime will not decreases and incorrigible offenders would continue their depredations on the people."

The following list shows who were reconvicted during the year 1884–85 under record :[87]

SUB - DIVISIONS	Name of followers	Crime	Remarks
Sudder sub – division	Kalta Nashya	Sec. 380 I P.C.	After two previous convictions in cases under section 386 and 353 was sentenced to 2 and half months rigorous imprisonment under section 380 I.P.C in the present case
Ditto	Tari Nashya	Sec. 379 I.P.C.	Previously case convicted under section 380 I.P.C. was sentenced in the present case to 1 months rigorous imprisonment under section 379 I.P.C.
Ditto	Pagla Das	Sec. 379 I.P.C.	Convicted once under section 379 I.P.C. and was sentenced in the present case to 5 days rigorous imprisonment under section 379 I.P.C.
Mathabhnaga Sub - division	Krista Dass	Sec. 380 I.P.C.	Once convicted before under section 457, I.P.C. and was sentenced in the present case to 5 months rigorous imprisonment under section 380 I.P.C.

During the year under report only one sword and one *Bhote–chora* were seized by the police against nil in the previous year.[88] 52 license were taken out against 53 in the preceding year. Mr. C.E. Briscoe appointed as an Assistant Superintendent of Police for the State.[89]

Thus the monarchical force was set an example of modern means of systematic law and order system under the Maharaja.

NOTES AND REFERENCES

1. *A.A.R of the C.B.S. (1878–79),* p. 39.
2. *Ibid.*
3. *Ibid.*
4. *Ibid.*
5. *Ibid.*
6. *Loc.cit.*
7. *Ibid.*
8. *Ibid.*
9. *Ibid.*
10. *Ibid.*
11. *Ibid.*, p. 40.
12. *Ibid.*
13. *Ibid.*
14. *Ibid.*
15. *Ibid.*
16. *Ibid.*
17. *Loc.cit.*
18. *Loc.cit.*
19. *Ibid.*, p. 41.
20. *Ibid.*
21. *Ibid.*
22. *Ibid.*
23. *Ibid.*
24. *Ibid.*
25. *Ibid.*
26. *Ibid.*
27. *Ibid.*, p. 42.

28. *Ibid.*
29. *A.A.R. of the C.B.S (1879–80),* p. 35.
30. *Ibid.*
31. *Ibid.*
32. *Ibid.*, p. 36.
33. *Ibid.*
34. *Ibid.*
35. *Loc.cit.*
36. *Ibid.*
37. *Ibid.*
38. *Ibid.*
39. *Ibid.*, p. 37.
40. *Ibid.*
41. *Ibid.*
42. *Ibid.*
43. *Ibid.*
44. *A.A.R. of the C.B.S (1883–84),* p. 16.
    (a) The decrease of Rs. 1.74 is due to the reduced contribution paid under Government orders on account of Superintendent Police's pension.
    (b) This amount was due to the appointment of an Assistant Superintendent of Police in December last.
    (c) The increase of Rs. 3,336 was due to an increase of Rs. 1 in the pay of 265 constables and also to 13 men having obtained good conduct allowances of Rs.1.
45. *Ibid.*
46. *Ibid.*
47. *Ibid.*
48. *Loc.cit.*, p. 17.
49. *Loc.cit.*
50. *Ibid.*
51. *Ibid.*

52. *Ibid.*, p. 18.
53. *Ibid.*
54. *Loc.cit.*
55. *Ibid.*
56. *Ibid.*
57. *Ibid.*
58. *Ibid.*
59. *Loc.cit.*, p. 19.
60. *Ibid.*
61. *Ibid.*
62. *Ibid.*
63. *Ibid.*
64. *Ibid.*, p. 20.
65. *Loc.cit.*
66. *Ibid.*
67. *Ibid.*
68. A.A.R. of the C.B.S (1884–85), p. 8.
69. *Ibid.*
70. *Ibid.*, p. 10.
71. *Ibid.*
72. *Ibid.*
73. *Ibid.*
74. *Ibid.*
75. *Ibid.*
76. *Ibid.*, p. 11.
77. *Loc.cit.*
78. *Loc.cit.*
79. *Ibid.*
80. *Ibid.*
81. *Ibid.*
82. *Ibid.*
83. *Ibid.*, p. 12.

84. *Ibid.*
85. *Ibid.*
86. *Ibid.*, p. 13.
87. *Ibid.*
88. *Ibid.*, p. 14.
89. *Ibid.*

3

Reviewing the Old System of Management

The State of Cooch Behar represents a systematic management of law and order in the 19th Century Bengal. During the period custody of the State was a notable thing to discuss. The charge of the Jail throughout the year rested with the *Fauzdari Ahilkar*, Babu Jadab Chander Chackerbutty. The jail wall, which was commenced in 1877–78 has during the year under report been nearly completed. As before stated the work has been done almost entirely by jail labour and has therefore progressed but slowly.[1]

The site of the existing hospital being out - side the wall, preparations have been made for its removal and reconstruction on one side of the large tank inside. On the completion of the wall some redistribution of the present *cutcha* wards will be necessary, so as to separate the civil and *hajut* prisoners more effectually than has as yet been feasible and also so as to minimize the risk from fire.[2]

The Commissioner during his last visit thought that of a *pucca* guard house and office should be constructed outside the wall, abutting on to it, on either side of the principal gate. Estimates are being prepared.

Disposal of the prisoners in the Sudder Jail :[3]

DISPOSAL OF PRISONERS IN THE SUDDER JAIL	1877–78	1878–79
Died	5	7
Escaped	1	3
Released	519	766
Transfered	17	5
Remaining in the jail on the last day of the year	347	205

The Statement in the margin will show the disposal of the prisoners in the year under report, as compared with the preceding year. Seven deaths occurred against five in the preceding year.[4] There was no cholera up to the close of the year, though the Superintendent regret to say that during the current month (April) cholera has made its appearance and carried off about a dozen prisoners. Of three escapes against one in the previous year, two were by prisoners at outdoor work in the Nilcoti and one from the jail garden. The escaping prisoners were all men with less than six months to serve and the escapes were due to over confidence and carelessness on the part of the warders who have been tried and punished. No offender was sentenced to transportation during the year, nor was any lunatic transferred to Dacca.[5]

Health of prisoners : The health of the prisoners during the year was not so good as in 1877–78. The ratio of admissions to Hospital, per cent of average strength was 31.8 against 24.97 and that of the daily average number of sick was 4.46 against 4.3. The mortality from cholera was 2 or less than one per cent. Of the 7 deaths, 2 only were from cholera, 2 from general debility, 1 from dysentery, 1 from enlargement of spleen and 1 from colic pain. Full particulars regarding sickness there has been Dr. Briscoe's medical report.[6]

Description	1877-78	1878-79
Average population of the Sudder Jail	251	224
Admission on account of sickness	232	314
Average sick	10.004	10.07
Percentage of admission to population	24.7	31.8
Average sick per cent of average population	4.3	4.46
Deaths	5	7
Death rate to 100 prisoners	2	3

Labour and manufacture : The prisoners were chiefly employed building the *pucca* masonry wall round the Jail. The cleared the jungle of the town, worked under the Public Works Department and the Artizan's school and in the Printing Press. The number that work in the Printing Press daily has been increased from 11 to 14. The jail garden supplied employment for those who were either old, convalescent or otherwise considered unfit for hard work.[7] The number of men employed in manufactures was a little more than that in the previous year, viz. 45 against 40. The principal branches of manufactures in which prisoners were employed were carpentry sawing wood, mat making weaving and twine making, making *soorkee*, grinding flour and baking bread. A number of man were also employed as jail servants, viz, convict warders, water carriers, cooks, sweepers and hospital settlements.[8]

The officer in charge thinks that " petty manufactures are not so profitable as one or two suitable industries" and he is anxious to introduce, more largely, oil pressing as a labour.. If this pays well there can be no possible objection to it, but rather the contrary, as oil pressing is first class labour and it has been inclined to think that convicts have as a rule too easy times of it and do not find the routine of jail life so unpleasant as is desirable that they should.[9]

The gross earnings of the laboring prisoners during the past and the preceding years will be found in the Statement given below :[10]

Description	1877 - 78			1878 - 79			Reference to Statement C
	Rs	As.	P.	Rs.	As.	P.	
Jail servant @ Rs 4 - 11 per mensem	1,641	14	0	1,553	2	0	Column 5.
Repairing Jail	140	15	0	310	2	6	Column 6.
On the roads, jail Wall &c.	3,110	0	0	3,143	2	0	Column 7.
Working for hire @ Rs.5 - 10	478	15	0	225	14	0	Column 8.
On the Jail garden @ Rs.57 - 8 in 1877 - 78 and @ Rs.53 - 6 - 3 in 1878 - 79 per head per annum..	747	3	3	747	6	1	Column 11.
On manufacture @ Rs. 114 in 1877 - 78 and Rs.71 - 9 - 8 in 1878 - 79	4,669	7	0	5,223	5	11	Column 12.
Total	10,988	11	3	9,208	2	6	

The gross earnings of the past year are less than those of the preceding year by Rs. 1780 – 8 – 9. This was attributable to two causes : First to the reduction in the number of prisoners, the daily average of which was 224 in the year under report against 231 of the preceding year;

and secondly to the fact that a very large number of prisoners were engaged during the year on the masonry wall which work was less profitable than brick–making in which the greater number of prisoners in 1877–78 were employed.[11]

The gross earnings per head of prisoners employed in the Jail garden has fallen from Rs. 57 – 8 to Rs. 53 – 6. This was due, regret to State, to the complete failure of an attempt to grow tobacco in the garden under Senor Montfort's supervision; unfortunately worms appeared and destroyed the entire crop.[12] New plants were substituted for those which died, but to no purpose and the result was that the labour of a considerable useless and plantation for above and ever was entirely wasted. Some remarkably fine potatoes were grown in the Jail garden this year, better than any have seen brought from Buxa of Darjeeling.[13]

The prisoners employed in manufacture have corned Rs. 71 – 9 – 8 per head against Rs. 144 in the previous year, owing to the fact that the construction of the wall comes under this head and building was far less profitable than brick making. Properly speaking the work of the two years should be taken together and an average struck to ascertain the real value of the work of each.[14]

The earnings of the jail during the last year were Rs. 7,314 – 14 (vide statement B) against Rs. 9,205 -14 – 3 showing a decrease of Rs. 1,861 – 0 – 3. The reasons to which this falling off is attributable have been given in detail in the foregoing paragraph under the head of gross earnings.[15]

EXPENDITURE	1877 – 78			1878 – 79		
	Rs.	As.	P.	Rs.	As.	P.
Police guard	2,656	3	3	3,210	6	3
Establishment	3,115	13	0	3,100	2	0
Feeding	8,907	10	6	10,262	9	3
Contingent	358	7	6	555	13	9
Clothing and blankets	1,054	13	0	915	13	0
Jail building and repairs	300	0	0	379	13	3
Gross cost	15,802	15	3	18,425	9	6
Deduct profits on manufacture, &c.	9,205	14	3	7,344	14	0
Net cost	7,597	4	0	11,080	11	6
Average gross cost of each prisoner	72	11	10	82	4	1
Average net cost of each prisoner	32	14	2	49	7	5

The above statement shows a very large increase in the gross and net cost of jail for the year under review as compared with the preceding and a still larger proportionate increase in the gross and net cost of each prisoner. Notwithstanding that the average population of the jail during the year was 224 against 231 of that proceeding the gross cost of 1878–79 was Rs. 27 more than that of 1877–78. The gross cost of each prisoner exceeds that of the former year by Rs. 10 and the net cost by Rs. 17 nearly.[16]

This large increased cost is due to the following causes :[17]

Firstly: An increase of Rs. 554 in cost of jail guard due to the necessity of an extra guard for the Hospital which was outside the masonry wall during the year under report.

Secondly: An increase of Rs. 1,354 – 14 – 9 under the head "feeding". Notwithstanding the fact that there were fewer months to feed, prices ruled so high that an extra grant of Rs. 3,000 had to be applied for beyond the amount estimated and sanctioned in the budget. Rice sold at Rs. 6 – 4 for good and Rs. 5 for common sorts at one period of the year.

Thirdly: The decrease in the gross profits of the prisoners' labour, which go to diminish the gross cost of the Jail.

The details of the gross cost of each prisoner are given in the sub–joined table. It will be seen that it is only under diet and jail guard that there is any noticeable difference while a decrease is shown under some heads.[18]

YEAR	JAIL GUARD			ESTABLISHMENT			DIET			Clothing and bedding			Building and repairing jail			Medicine and contingencies		
1877–78	11	8	0	13	7	10	38	9	0	4	9	0	2	3	1	2	7	0
1878–79	14	5	4	13	13	5	45	15	0	4	1	6	1	12	2	2	7	8

The amount actually remitted to the treasury Rs. 9,263 – 3 – 2 against Rs. 10,933 of the preceding year and Rs. 5,100 – 10 – 11 of the year 1876 – 77. The preceding year 1877 – 78 was an exceptional one in as much that the attention of the whole establishment was wholly concentrated on brick making and all the available prisoners were employed at it.[19]

The amount remitted consisted of the following items :

	Rs.	A.	P.
Earnings of out–door labour hired out to Public Works Department	2,257	4	2
Sale proceeds of garden produce....................	864	13	4
Sale proceeds of articles manufactured in the preceding year	2,906	3	6
Do. Do in the year under report.......................	3,232	5	8
Found with prisoners and confiscated....................	2	8	6
Total	9,263	3	2

Besides this amount Rs. 27 – 4 – 3 were remitted to the Treasury on account of the earnings of the prisoners at Mekhligunj.[20]

The earnings of convicts employed in out–door work for the state are shown only on paper. The number of prisoners admitted into the three Lock–ups at Dinhata, Mathabhnaga and Mekhligunj during the year under report was 481 against 442 of the preceding year, showing an increase of 39 men. 57 men remained in the lock – ups at the close of the preceding year; out of the total number, 143 were transferred to the Sudder Jail and different Lock-ups 1 died, 5 escaped, 357 were released and 32 remained at the close of the year. The cost of feeding in the Lock–ups was Rs. 51 – 9 against Rs. 45 – 8 – 6 showing an increase of Rs. 6 – 0 – 6, per head. This is owing to the high price of the articles of food which prevailed during the year under report.[21]

The Mathabhanga Lock–up is threatened by the river which has approached to within a few feet. It will probably be necessary to remove it this year in order to avoid it being washed away. The general conduct of the prisoners throughout the year was good.[22]

The charge of the jail rested with Babu Satya Charan Mookerjee, officiating *Fouzdari Ahilkar*, from the beginning of the year up to the 15th September 1880 and with the *Fouzdari Ahilkar* from the 16th idem to the end of the year.[23]

Two new kitchens with galvanized iron roofs, lath plaster walls and masonry floors and the civil *hajut* and female wards, all of which were under construction at the end of the previous year were completed during the year under report.[24] The kitchens were a very great improvement upon the old kitchen huts in as much as they are secure from fire. These were made entirely by prison labour. The two pucca buildings on the two sides of the jail entrance were also completed by the Public Works department during the year. The one to the North has been occupied by the guard and the other to the south was used for the jailor's office and the store–room.[25]

Disposal of Prisoners: The disposal of prisoners in the Sudder jail during the year as compared with that of the previous year will be found in the statement given below:[26]

Disposal of the Prisoners in the Sudder jail	*1879–80*	*1880–81*
Died	21	4
Escaped	8	1
Released	660	575
Transferred	14	18
Remaining in the Jail on the last day of the year	175	209

The number of deaths was 4 against 21 of the preceding year, showing a decrease of 17. Of the 4 deaths one was from diarrhea, one from dysentery, one from fever and from pneumonia. There was only one escape during the year against eight of the previous year.[27] The escaped prisoner one Jonaku Nosya was convicted in a theft case and sentenced to two year's rigorous imprisonment in August 1879. The man had only four months and thirteen days to serve out. He was working in the jail garden and was deputed to keep an eye on the goats (purchased for the use of the prisoner) grazing about the garden. He was in the custody of warders of the jail garden who were also prisoners.[28] These warders were prosecuted in the criminal courts, convicted and punished with imprisonment under section 223 of the Indian Penal Code. Measures have been adopted for the recapture of the escaped prisoner. The man is a resident of Bhatabari, a village in the Jalpaiguri district and there will. Therefore, he some difficulty, in recapturing him.[29] As escaped convict by name Heera Singh, a Punjabi by birth, who was convicted in a dacoity case in Cooch Behar and sentenced to rigorous imprisonment for 10 years, escaped from the Cooch Behar jail in 1865; i.e about 16 years ago. The man went to Pubna and took service under the lord *Zamindars*. His whereabouts were ascertained and a warrant was sent to the Magistrate of Pabna for his arrest. He was undergoing imprisonment in the Pubna Jail, having been convicted in a theft cause.[30] He was however; sent up there on the expiry of his term of imprisonment during the year under report. He is a most daring character and will be sent to the Alipore Jail when an opportunity offers. The Bengal Government (letter No. 2524, dated December 10th 1880, Political Department, to the address of the Commissioner of the Rajshayee and Cooch Behar Division) sanctioned the transfer of long term prisoners from the Cooch Behar state Jail to the Alipore Jail on payment of Rs. 50 per annum for the maintenance of the each person.[31] Advantage was taken of this order to end down 13 prisoners, all notorious bad characters, to the Alipore Jail on the 5th March last. Besides these, one man, a lunatic was sent to the asylum to Dacca for treatment. Properly speaking there were only 14 transfer but 4 often were sent to Sub–divisions and if these be added to this number the total transfer is 18 against 14 of the previous year.[32]

Health of prisoners: The table given below compares the return of sickness and mortality in the Jail for the post and preceding years :[33]

Description	**1879–80**	**1880–81**
1. Average Population of the Sudder Jail	191	166
2. Admission on account of sickness	262	191
3. Average sick	10.4	6.2
4. Percentage of admission to population	29.8	31.1
5. Average sick percent of average population	5.2	2.6
6. Deaths	21	4
7. death rate to 100 prisoners	10	2

It will be seen that the past year has been a remarkably healthy one as far as the population of the jail was concerned. The death rate percent has come down 10 to 2. There was no case of cholera or any other epidemic disease during the year.[34]

Labour and manufacture : The prisoners were employed in clearing the jungle in the town, working under the Public Works Department and Printing Press. The Jail garden supplied employment for those who were other old, convalescent or otherwise considered unfit for hard work.[35]

The number of men employed in manufactures was more than that in the previous year viz., 39 against 34. The principal manufactures in which the prisoners were employed were carpentry, sawing wood, mat making, weaving, wine – making, grinding flour, baking bread and pressing oil. Many prisoners were also employed as jail servants viz; convict warders, water carriers, cooks, weepers and hospital attendants.[36]

Gross Earnings: The Gross earnings of the laboring prisoners during the past and the preceding years will be found in the following statement :[37]

DESCRIPTION	1879 – 80			1880 – 81			Reference to statement C
	Rs	A.	P.	Rs	A.	P	
Jail servants at Rs. 4 – 11 as per mensem ------	1,781	1	5	1,459	1	0	Column V
Repairing the Jail ------------------------------	337	5	0	171	4	0	Column VI
On the roads &c. --------------------------------	2,055	12	6	1,458	8	3	Column VII
Working for hire at Rs. 5 - 10 per mensem ------	122	10	0	170	13	0	Column VIII
On the jail garden at Rs 59 – 12 – 4 in 1879 – 80 And at Rs. 68 – 2 – 8 in 1880 – 81 per head Per annum	536	4	5	613	6	2	Column XI
On manufacture at Rs. 89 – 12 – 7 in 1879 – 80 And at Rs. 127 – 8 – 8 in 1880 – 81 per head Per annum	3,052	12	7	4,175	10	9	Column XII
Total --------------	7,887	12	0	8,028	13	2	

The gross earnings of the past year exceeded those of the preceding year by Rs. 141 – 1 – 2. It will be observed that the gross earnings per head of prisoners employed in the Jail garden have risen from Rs. 59 – 12 – 11 to Rs. 68 – 2 – 8 and the prisoners employed in manufactures have earned Rs. 127 – 8 – 8 per head against Rs. 89 – 12 – 7 in the previous year.[38] These figures are satisfactory and creditable to the Officer in charge Babu Jadab Chandra Chuckerbutty.[39]

The net earnings of the jail during the year under report were Rs. 6,398 – 8 – 2 against Rs. 5,769 – 7 – 6 showing an increase of Rs. 629 – 0 – 8. Considering the falling off in the number of prisoners the result was satisfactory.[40]

The Statement given below will show the gross and the net cost of the Jail as also of each prisoner during the past and the preceding years:[41]

ON ACCOUNT OF	1879 – 80			1880 – 81		
	Rs.	A.	P.	Rs.	A.	P.
1. Police guard	3,557	1	0	2,332	5	6
2. Establishment	3,166	15	0	3,105	13	3
3. Feeding	8,274	8	3	5,538	8	0
4. Contingencies	535	1	3	539	10	0
5. Clothing and bedding	834	3	3	641	4	0
6. Jail building and repairs	517	0	0	538	15	6
Gross cost	16,682	7	3	13,455	8	3
Deduct profit of manufacture &c.	5,769	7	5	6,398	8	10
Net cost	10,913	0	3	7,057	15	5
	87	5	5	81	0	1
	57	2	2	42	8	3

The gross cost shows a decrease of Rs. 3,225 – 15 – 6 and the net cost of Rs. 3,855 – 0 – 10. There is also a decrease in the gross and the net cost of each prisoner. The former from Rs. 87 – 5 – 5 to 80 – 0 – 0 and the later from Rs. 57 – 2 – 2 to Rs. 42 – 8 – 3. The details of the gross cost of each prisoner in the jail in the past year as compared with those of the preceding year were given in the table below :[42]

YEAR	Jail guard			Establishment			Diet			Clothing and bedding			Building and repairs			Medicine and contingencies		
	Rs		A.	Rs	A.	P.	Rs.	A.	P.	Rs	A.	P.	Rs.	A.	P.	Rs	A.	P.
1879 – 80	[illegible]			16	9	0	45	5	1	4	5	11	1	11	3	2	12	9
1880 – 81	17	9	2	16	11	4	35	15	5	3	13	9	5	6	1	3	6	6
	17	10	0															

Remittance to the treasury : The amount remitted to the Treasury during the year was Rs. 7,338 against 8,797 – 10 – 8 of the preceding year, showing a decrease of Rs. 1,345 – 10 – 8. The permanent jailor fell seriously ill during the latter end of the year and was obliged to take six months medical leave. His officiating incumbent was an entirely new man and failed to collect the amount of the jail manufacture bills. They were being realized by the *Fouzdari Ahilkar* itself.[43]

The details of remittance were given below:[44]

	Rs.	A.	P.
1. Earnings of out–door labor employed by the Public Works Department	285	14	4
2. Sale Proceeds of garden produce and of articles manufactured	7,003	13	11
3. Earnings of out – door labor hired out to private parties	48	8	9
Total	7,338	0	0

The number of prisoners admitted into the three lock–ups of Mathabhanga, Dinhata and Mekhligunj during the year under report was 325 against 365 of the preceding year, showing a decrease of 40 prisoners.[45] Thirty–nine prisoners remained in the Lock–ups at the close of the previous year. Out of the total number 364, 69 were transferred to the Sudder jail, one died, one escaped 289 were released and 12 remained at the close of the year.[46] The cost of the feeding &c. of each prisoner in the Lock–ups was Rs. 38 – 5 – 8 against Rs. 45 – 3 – 3 in the previous year, showing a decrease of Rs. 6 -13 – 7 per head. This is owing to the fall in the price of articles of food during the year. The lock–up at Mathabhanga together with the greater portion of the civil Station was washed away by the river Jaldhaka during the year under report. It has been removed to a safe place about half a mile distant.[47]

General Conduct of prisoners has been on the whole better than that in the previous year. Two men only had to be flogged and three lost their marks for breach of jail rules and discipline &c.[48]

The introduction of the mark system in the jail has been productive of marked good among the prisoners, who fully appreciate the advantages of it and do their best to behave themselves properly.[49] During the year under report two prisoners named Nabir Nasya and Wuzir Nasya, dacoits, who were sentenced to four years rigorous imprisonment for committing dacoits, who were sentenced to four years rigorous imprisonment for committing dacoit, obtained remission of sentences by seven and eight weeks respectively.[50] Special marks for excellence of workmanship, unusual industry and success in teaching carpentry were awarded to the prisoner Asarh Das under Section 338 of the jail rules.[51]

Arrangement for educating some of the young prisoners have been made in the jail from the month of January last and a class consisting of nine prisoners has been formed for the purpose.[52] An intelligent and well-behaved prisoner with a fair knowledge of the Bengali language has been appointed teacher. Simple instruction in reading, writing and arithmetic has been given. The school sits for two hours every morning in one of the wards of the jail.[53]

Great credit was due to Babu Jadub chunder Chukerbutty for his energy and ability in the management of the jail.[54]

In 1883 regarding the sickness and mortality in the jail, Dr. Briscoe reports as follows :

The following table shows the sickness and mortality as compared with the daily strength for the past two years:[55]

YEAR	Average daily strength	PERCENTAGE OF STRENGTH			REMARKS
		Admissions	Deaths	Daily sick	
1862 - 63	187.54	76.7	2.12	3.72	
1861 - 62	213.5	112.2	2.81	3.34	

The above shows the daily average strength of prisoners to be nearly 26 less than that of the preceding year, with a decrease of 33.5 per cent in the sick rate and 0.69 in the mortality. Out of 160 cases treated including 12 remaining from the previous year, 63 were malarious fever, ague and remittent, 15 diarrhea, 7 rheumatism and 5 respiratory affections.[56]

Four deaths occurred, three from dysentery and one remitted fever. Fevers were most prevalent during May, September and November and bowel complaints in May and October.[57]

The healthiest months were June and July 1882, January and February 1883 daily average sick percent of strength being in these months 3.86, 3.69, 1.9 and 2.35 respectively. The most unhealthy months were April and May giving a daily average of 4.67 and 5.73 respectively.[58]

Dr. Briscoe records two cases of snake bite, occurring among prisoners in out – door work, which were successfully treated by him after Dr. Vincent Richard's plan; viz ligature with injection of the Permanganate of potash.[59] Unfortunately the value of these cases from a therapeutic point of view was lessened by the fact that in neither case was the snake caught and though from the punctures visible there was no doubt that the men were bitten by a snake of some kind, it is not certain what snake it was and whether more or less poisonous.[60]

The sanitary condition of the jail was to be good one. The dry earth system in the latrines was carried out effectually and the night soil buried in trenches out -side the jail. The food was always found to be of good quality well cooked and sufficiently varied. The drinking water was brought on carts from the Sagardighee.[61]

The following statement shows the sickness and mortality for the past two years :[62]

YEAR	POLICE				MILITARY			
	PER CENT OF STRENGTH				PER CENT OF STRENGTH			
	Daily average strength	Admissions	Deaths	Daily average sick	Daily average strength	Admissions	Deaths	Daily sick
1882 – 83	267	57.94	0.35	1.74	137	124	2.19	3.08
1881 - 82	305	74.22	0.35	1.85	136	138.23	----	3.98

In the military there was a decrease of 14 per cent in the admissions on the preceding year and nearly seven in the Police, but as usual the admissions among the military were nearly double that of the Police. Men from the North–west cannot stand the climate of Cooch Behar.[63]

The total number of Police and Military treated including 12 remaining from the previous year was 373 of which 259 suffered from malarias fever, ague and remittent; 22 dysentery, 17 diarrhea, 13 respiratory affections and 11 rheumatism. Three deaths occurred among the Military, two from Pneumonia and one from spleen. Police, one death from general debility and dyspepsia.[64]

Native Doctor Hurry Charan Sen was attached to the jail, police and military hospitals. He has good professional abilities and performed his duties to the Civil Surgeon's entire satisfaction.[65]

The charge of the jail throughout the year rested with the *Fouzdari Ahilkar*. Regarding jail building it need to include that one additional room for storing Provisions and one solitary cell were built during the year under report. The work has been done entirely by the Public Works Department. The jail buildings were kept in good repair throughout the year.[66]

The statement given below compares the disposal of prisoners during the past and previous years.[67]

Disposal of prisoners in the sudder jail	1902–03	1903–04
Died	4	13
Escaped	1	3
Released	535	526
Transferred	7	10
Remaining in the jail on the last day of the year	205	158

There were 13 deaths in the year under report, against 4 in the previous year. Of these 9 were from cholera, 2 from remittent fever, 1 from pneumonia and 1 from heart disease. The number of escapes was 3 against 1 in the previous year; they happened as follows :[68] Prisoner Jhagru Nashya, while marking bricks in the brick–field under a convict warder kharua Das, took advantage of the warder's carelessness and made his escape. He is a resident of Buldeh, a village in Fulcoomrah Station in Rangpore and was convicted of retaining possession of stolen property and sentenced to 2 and half years rigorous imprisonment of which he had undergone only 8 days. The convict warder was degraded and the two peons who were primarily responsible were judicially tried and fined. All that could be done was done for retaking the convict. Warrants were yet out and Tufangunj Police have been specially ordered to interest themselves in the matter. Second case, prisoners Biroo Das and Debu Das were sent to work in the Civil Surgeon's garden. They were under the charge of a convict warder Gauri Kanth Das who being obliged to go to the river bank to relieve nature, left the prisoners in the garden to take care of themselves. The prisoners taking advantage of the warder's absence, made their escape. Both the prisoners were convicted in theft cases and were sentenced to 2 years and 11 month's rigorous imprisonment each, of which they had under gone only 2 months and 13 days. These prisoners have since been recaptured. The convict warder through whose negligence the escape occurred was judicially tried and sentenced to additional imprisonment for 3 months. Both the escaped prisoners have been judicially tried and each sentenced to undergo rigorous imprisonment for one year under Section 224 of the Indian Penal Code. 10 prisoners were transferred during the last year against 7 of the previous year. Of these 4 were transferred to Jalpaiguri for release and remaining 6 (life prisoners) to Alipore jail for deportation to Port Blair. 158 Prisoners remained in jail the last day of the year against 205 of the preceding year.

The sub–joined table compares the returns of sickness and mortality in the jail during the past and previous years [69]

Description	1882–83	1883–84
Average population of the sudder jail	187	166.77
Admission on account of sickness ——	148	233
Average sick ——	6.9	6.15
Percentage of admission to population —	19	32
Average sick – percentage of average population	3.2	3.6
Deaths ——	4	13
Deaths rate to 100 prisoners ——	2	7

The health of the prisoners during the year was not so good as in 1882 – 83. Cholera broke out in an epidemic form throughout the State and carried off thousands of people. It afterwards made its appearance in the jail during the months of may and June. 21 prisoners were attacked with the disease of whom 9 died and 12 were cured. Had it not been for the very excellent arrangement made by Dr. Briscoe, the number of deaths would doubtless have been greater.[70]

Temporary wards were erected outside the jail wall and to receive patients suffering from cholera and the services of an additional compounder were entertained and the Civil surgeon spent a good deal of his time with the patients. All the wards were constantly fumigated with sulfur and coal tar and greatest possible attention was paid to every detail in regard to the diet &c., of the prisoners.[71]

The branches of industry in which the prisoners were employed during the year under report were carpentry sawing wood, tailoring, flour grinding, baking bread, gunny making, pressing oil and the manufacture of rugs, durries, towels, dusters, twine and bamboo furniture. They were also employed in clearing the jungle in the town and under the Public Works Department and the printing press.[72] The convalescent and those who were found unfit for hard work, were employed in the jail garden. Prisoners were also employed as jail servants i.e convict warders, water – carriers, cooks, sweepers and hospital attendants.[73]

The comparative statement given below will show the gross earnings during the past and previous years :[74]

Description	1882 – 83			1883 – 84		
	Rs.	A.	P.	Rs.	A.	P.
Jail servants @ Rs. 4 - 11 per mensem	1,582	13	0	1,603	9	6
Repairing the jail	57	8	0	44	8	5
On roads and Printing Press	1,788	12	0	1,422	15	0
Hired out to outsiders @ Rs. 5 - 10	419	4	0	279	5	0
Jail garden @ Rs. 54 – 1 - 5 in 1882 - 83 and @ Rs. 41 – 8 – 9 in 1883 – 84	432	11	9	332	5	6
On manufacture @ Rs. 53 – 13 – 5 in 1882 – 83 and @ Rs. 30 – 11 – 6 in 1883 – 84	2,045	15	10	1,075	14	2
Total	6,326	14	7	4,758	9	8

The gross earnings of the year under report were Rs. 4,758 – 9 – 8 against Rs. 6,326 – 14 – 7 of the preceding year, showing decrease in the number of laboring prisoners during the year.[75] The daily average population in the jail and that of laboring prisoners were 166 and 131 against 187 and 147 respectively in the previous year showing a decrease of 21 and 16 prisoners. The average daily number of prisoners employed in manufacture was only 35 against 38 of the preceding year. The number employed during the year was therefore less than that in the previous year.[76] It will be observed that the earnings of each prisoner employed in the garden and manufacture were shorter than those of the previous years, by 12 and 23 rupees respectively. This was accounted for by the following facts :[77]

"1stly; For more than a month during the Installation, the prisoners employed in the above industries had to be constantly told off in the midst of their work to the Nilkuthi and Rajbari.

2ndly; Formerly indigenous wheat used to be mixed up with Patna wheat in making bread. It was found that this practice went to deteriorate the quality of bread. Patna wheat was therefore exclusively used in the baking, so that had to pay Rs. 1,743 for the price of wheat in the place of Rs. 887 only paid in the previous year. This fact went to a great extent to lower the profits of manufacture."

The net earnings of the jail during the year under report were Rs. 3,098 – 14 – 8 against Rs. 4,744 -1 – 7 of the preceding year; showing a decrease of Rs. 1,645 – 2 – 11; such kind of decrease, owing to a corresponding decrease in the number of prisoners employed in manufactures in the year under report.[78]

The amount remitted to the treasury during the year was Rs. 6647 – 13 – 9 against Rs. 4,293 – 8 – 3 of the previous year, showing an increase of Rs. 2,354 – 5 – 6. This was attributable to the fact that pressure was put upon the practice who were indebted to the jail. The British administration came to an end in October 1883 and great efforts were made to release arrears.[79]

The following table shows the gross and net cost of the jail as also of each prisoner during the past and preceding years:[80]

On account of	1882 – 83			1883 – 84		
Police guard	2,619	5	0	2,566	8	0
Establishment	3,060	12	9	3,338	8	3
Feeding	6,810	4	9	6,039	14	0
Contingencies	543	10	3	966	1	9
Clothing and bedding	834	7	0	815	3	6
Jail buildings and repairs	348	0	3	464	7	8
Gross cost	14,321	6	0	14,240	11	2
Deduct earnings &c.	4,744	1	7	4,756	9	8
Net cost	9,577	4	5	9,482	1	6

The gross cost of the jail during the past year has decreased by Rs. 80 – 9 – 10 and the net cost by Rs. 95 – 2 - 11. The police guard alone cost a large sum. This expenditure, properly speaking, should not be shown here as it has been already shown in the reports. The warder system has been introduced in some of the Government jails in Bengal as an experimental measure and it has proved fairly successful. Regarding the *Fouzdary Ahilkar* remarks :[81] "I should very much like to come up with a proposition to introduce the system here in our jail and thus try to effect a saving under this head." There has been an increase of Rs. 277 - 11 - 6 under the head establishment. This was owing to the fact that an increase was sanctioned to the pay of the *Naib* Jailor and some of the warders from 1st December last. The outbreak of cholera in the jail in May last made it necessary to build 2 temporary cholera wards out -side the jail compound.[82] A large number of blankets, bedding and articles of clothing had to be destroyed and new ones purchased. Besides these extra sweeper had to be engaged. These and many other things swelled the expenditure under the head "contingencies" which was greater than that of the previous by Rs. 319 – 7 – 6.

The Statement given below compares the details of the gross cost of each prisoner in the jail during the year under report with those of the preceding year :[83]

		Year					
		1882 – 83			1883 – 84		
Jail guard	Rs.	14	0	1	15	7	4
Establishment	Rs.	15	5	10	20	1	9
Diet	Rs.	35	6	8	35	11	5
Clothing and bedding	Rs.	4	7	7	4	14	4
Building and repairs	Rs.	1	13	9	2	12	9
Medicines and contingencies	Rs.	5	7	5	5	13	3

The little increase in the diet of the prisoners was owing to the fact that the thing was dearer than during last year.

The *Fouzdari Ahilkar* reports as follows regarding the lock-ups :[84]

"The number of prisoners admitted into the three lockups of Dinhata, Mathabhanga and Mekhligunj during the year under report was 461 against 477 of the previous year showing a decrease of 16 prisoners. The number of admissions 461 added to 30 the number that remained in the lockups at the end of the previous year, gives a total number of 491. Out of this, 123 were transferred to the Sudder jail, 326 released, 1 died and 41 remained in the lockups at the close of the year. The cost per head of the prisoners in the lockups amounted to Rs. 35

-1 -10 against Rs. 36 – 7 – 8 in the previous year, showing a decrease of Rs. 1 – 5 – 10. The cost of feeding each prisoner in Mathabhanga has been so high as 44 – 7 – 9 against 40 – 13 – 7. The explanation that the price of rice was higher which was unsatisfactory. Considering that it was a Mufossil station, this cost should be much less. It was only Rs. 36 in the Sudder jail. The *Naib Ahilkar* has been asked to do all in his power to bring down the expenditure. With regard to the jail guard, the *Naib Ahilkar* writes " Unless the number of constables at the station was increased, the guards cannot be expected to be regular. Owing to the want of constables a sentry was not frequently required to be on duty for four or five hours continuously." As regards the jail buildings the *Naib Ahilkars* of Mathabhanga and Dinhata remarks :[85] "The bamboo checker of the lockup, if not the rooms as well, ought to be replaced by a *pucca* wall. Violent storms and then visit the sub–division and it was therefore not safe to depend upon the present checkers. I reported to you how a portion of the Sub -divisional *cutchery* was lately blown off at midnight by the thunderstorm and you can easily imagine in what a position should I have been placed, if the lockup checker had been blown down at the time of the night. It was fortunate that it was new, else it could not be proof against the storm of the night of the 24th March 1884." The lock up building has been erected more than 7 years ago. The ward rooms have become too old to ensure safe custody of prisoners. The whole building requires through renewal. The doors, gates etc. in short the wooden things should be replaced with new ones. The *Dewan*, I understood, has already been taken up the matter in hand and it was hoped that there will be *pucca* walls round the lock–up very soon. All the *Naib Ahilkar's* brought to my notice the very great difficulty they experiences in making the prisoners work outside the lock up. The guard of constables not only guard the Lock ups and are also in charge of the treasure chest. So it becomes impossible to send out prisoners to work. They propose to have a warder for every lock up. I think each lock up should have a warder to make the prisoners work outside the Lock up wall. In that case the public roads and the jungle in public places would be kept clean and small kitchen gardens near the lock ups would be opened out in which all kinds of vegetables (*Turkarees*) would grow, causing a great saving in the expenditure generally.[86]

The general conduct of prisoners has been on the whole better than that in the previous year. 4 prisoners were flogged, 4 got irons on their legs and 3 lost marks against 6 flogged, 1 put in irons and 7 who lost marks in the previous year.[87]

During the year 1883–84 under report 17 prisoners were released under the rules of the mark system against 8 of the previous year. The details were given ahead :[88]

No	Names of prisoners	Offences	Term of Imprisonment Period remitted under the mark system			Period remitted under the mark system	Date of release
			Year	M	D		
1	Shore Nashya	Section 395	10	-------	------	13 weeks	12th April 1883
2	Chamelie Teli	Neglect of duty	2	--------	------	6 weeks	19th April 1883
3	Pochamakra	Section 305	10	--------	------	18 weeks	10th May 1883
4	Golahari Das	Section 395	10	--------	-------	17 weeks	17th May 1883
5	Dola Das	Section 411	2	--------	------	5 weeks	9th July 1883
6	Sri Das	Section 395	10			3 weeks	4th Sept. 1883
7	Bhim Chand Nashya	Section 376	5	--------	------	16 weeks	20th Aug. 1883
8	Dobaria Das	Section 304	5	--------	------	7 weeks	10th Oct. 1883
9	Khir Das	Section 411	2	-------	------	9 weeks	1st Sept. 1883
10	Ram Mohan Das	Section 412	2	------	------	3 weeks	22nd Aug. 1883
11	Kunnaja Dehary Dose	Section 392	2	------	-----	10 weeks	1st Dec. 1883
12	Batul Nashva	Section 392	2	--------	------	8 weeks	16th Dec. 1883
13	Niasha Das	Section 457	1	--------	-------	5 weeks	21st Dec. 1883
14	Khotu Das	Section 376	4	-------	-------	14 weeks	21st Dec. 1883
15	Bhojo Das	Section 397	7			14 weeks	24th Dec. 1883
16	Chalo Das	Section 395	10	-------	------	18 weeks	16th Feb. 1883
17	Khudi Das	Section 395	10	------	------	21 weeks	26th Feb. 1883

With the sanction of Maharaja the 10 prisoners named below were released on the occasion of the installation of the Maharaja on the 9th November last year.

The Fouzdari Ahilkar reports as follows upon the conduct of State Police officers :[89]

> "Six head constables and 19 constables were judicially punished during the year under report against one Head constables of the previous year. Sub -inspector Gooru Prasanna Singha and ead constable Mahesh Chandra Raha deserve special mention as detective officers. Inspector Parbutty Charan Chakerbutty did good service in connection with a big dacoit case which took place in the jurisdiction of Shitai and sent up 12 men for trial. Almost the whole of the plundered property consisting of gold and silver ornaments have been recovered. Sub–Inspector Gooru Prasanna Singha deserves very great credit in successfully tracing out the Dacoits in the Nuldhoudra case which occurred in June 1883. Cholera was then raging most fearfully in the village so much so that in the house of the complainant alone 22 men had died of the disease and when only 3 surviving members of the complainant alone, 22 man had died of the disease and when only 3 surviving members

of the family were mourning over their deplorable circumstances, the ruffians took advantage of their misfortune and committed the dacoit. The Sub–Inspector manfully allowed his sense of duty to over–ride any fear of life and passed 2 or 3 days in the scene of death and disease. Some of his constables caught epidemic on the spot and died. The sub–Inspector himself very narrowly escaped, having had a few choleric motions himself after his return to the Station. I would respectfully recommend him for special reward for his admirable conduct in his case. The dacoits with one exception have all been convicted and sentenced to rigorous imprisonment by the Session Court."

"The police conducted themselves excellently well during the Installation. Thousands of people were assembled in the Town and the festivities went on for a whole week, but not a single case of theft or accident happened. 250 *chowkidars* were brought from the Mofussil and one half of the number was posted in all the parts of the Town and Nilkuti. The other half relieving the men at stated intervals. Mounted constables were made to go round the

> beats regularly and see that the men were in their respective posts. Sub – Inspector Gooru Prasanna Singh, Babu Sri Krishna Roy *Sheristadar* of the *Fouzdary* Court and *Naib Nazir* Giri Dhar Chakerbutty did good services in connection with the supply of milk, butter &c &c during the Installation. No less than 235 *maunds* of fresh milk, 147 *maunds* of dahee and khir, butter, sana &c &c were procured and supplied."

The amount of property stolen was Rs. 6,848 and recovered Rs. 1,863. The percentage of property recovered to property stolen was as 27.2. The remarks of the *Fouzdari Ahilkar* regarding unpunctuality and dilatoriness on the part of *Naib Ahilkars* show that these officers have not duly profited by the relief given them by an appointment of the Peripatetic *Naib Ahilkar* in the Civil Branch.[90]

In 1885 the charge of the sudder jail rested with the *Fouzdari Ahilkar* during the whole year except (from 7th February to 10th April 1885) when he went on privilege leave and the Superintendent of State Police officiated with him. In 1885, 6th June a violent gale blew down the wards No. 2 and 7 (*Dewani* ward). Both these wards were unoccupied at the time (5.30 p.m) and no one was hurt.[91]

The buildings were very old and the materials worn out. With the old material of the fallen wards No. 7 was rebuilt and an entirely new one built on the site of ward No. 2. The latter building was capable of accommodating 94 prisoners. The estimate was made by the Public Works Department and the work done by contract.[92] It was customary to give a house to the jailor. The late jailor had built one in the jail garden. It was burnt down on the 25th December; a new house will have to be erected for the present jailor in the course of the current year.[93]

The statement given below shows the disposal of the prisoners during the past year as compared with the previous year :[94]

Disposal of prisoners in the Sudder Jail	*1883–84*	*1884–85*
Died	13	6
Escaped	3	—
Released	526	565
Transferred	10	—
Remaining in the jail on the last day of the year	158	186

There were six deaths in the year under report against 13 in the previous year. Of these two were dysentery cases, one diarrhea, one fever, one Phthisis and one drowning in the tank within the jail wall.[95]

There were no escapes during the year. 186 prisoners were in the jail on the last day of the year against 158 of the preceding year.

The Sub–joined table compares the returns of sickness and mortality in the jail during the past and the preceding year :[96]

Description	1883–84	1884–85
Average population of the Sudder jail	166.77	177.71
Admission on account of sickness ——	233	221
Average sick ——	6.15	6.1
Death ——	13	6
Percentage of admission to population —	139.71	123.77
Average sick–percentage of average	3.69	3.43
Death–rate to 100 prisoners ——	7.79	3.37

The industries in which the prisoners were employed during the year under report were carpentry, brick – making, sawing flour grinding and in making gunny, durries, chicks, twine, bamboo and cane chairs, bamboo mats, cloth also in tailoring bakery, in the Printing Press and in the metal ling of the town roads under the Public Works Department. The convalescents and those unfit for hard labour were employed in the jail garden.[97] Certain prisoners were also employed as jail servants i.e convict warders, water-carriers, cooks, sweepers and hospital attendants. The average number of prisoners employed in jail manufactures was 43 against 35 of the previous year. The work of brick making commenced at the Bengchatra brick–fields from the 20th November last and continued till after the expiry of the official year.[98] The number of prisoners here employed was 7,285. Out of a total of 676,000 katcha bricks made in the season, 101,000 were damaged by rain. The balance 5,75,000 bricks were burnt. The out–turn was as under :[99]

	Rs.	A.	P.
1st Class 306,700 at Rs. 13 ———	3,987	1	3
2nd Class 82,275 at Rs. 10 ———	822	12	0
3rd Class 80,600 at Rs. 7 ———	564	3	2
Jhama 54,415 at Rs. 10 ———	544	0	0
523,990	5,918	0	5

The price of the bricks has been estimated Rs. 5,918 – 0 - 5. From this Rs. 3,981 – 6 – 0, as per memorandum given in the margin*, have to be deducted.[100]

Memo of expresses *

	Rs.	A.	P.
Coal 3,246 mds. @ 1 – 2 - 9	3804	7	6
Fuel 262 do. @ 0 – 4 – 0	65	8	0
Mistry ———	75	7	6
Bamboos ———	3	0	0
Mats 420 ———	13	12	0
Iron pans ———	4	11	0
Straw ———	3	0	0
Cooli hire at night ———	9	8	0
	3,981	6	0

The net profit was therefore, Rs. 1,936 – 10 - 5. Half the bricks have been sold already and the remainder will soon be similarly disposed off. Besides this above, 14,918 tiles have been burnt at a total cost of Rs. 742 – 11 – 6, viz. Rs. 58 – 9 - 6 the price of 50 *maunds* of coal, Rs. 372 the price of fuel, Rs. 11 – 4 for mats, Rs. 8 for hay, Rs. 4 for straw and Rs. 288 14 the wages of *mistrees*. The total value of the Tiles in stock, as shown in the margin * estimated at Rs. 750. About 45,000 *Katcha* Tiles were made but the soil being bad the outturn was also bad. The experiment has resulted in a net loss.[101]

The comparative statement given below shows the gross earnings during the past and previous years:[102]

Description	1883 – 84			1884 – 85		
	Rs.	A.	P.	Rs.	A.	P.
Jail servants @ Rs. 4 -11 per *mensem*	1,603	9	3	1,379	13	6
Repairing the Jail	44	3	6	135	5	0
On Printing Press	597	10	6	632	10	6
Metalling road	498	14	6	410	7	6
In the State Superintendent's garden	210	0	0	226	1	6
In the circuit bungalow garden	3	2	0	93	7	0
In the Civil Surgeon's garden	103	2	0	107	3	0
In the Private Secretary's garden	10	0	0	88	12	0
Hired out to outsiders @ Rs. 5 – 10 – 0	279	6	0	414	12	0
Jail garden @ 41 – 8 – 9 in 1883 – 84						
@ Rs. 36 – 1 -10 in 1884 – 85	382	6	6	433	5	0
On manufacture :						
At Rs. 30 – 11 – 6 in 1883 – 84 @ Rs. 45 – 0 – 7	1,075	14	2	1979	12	4
Total	4,758	9	3	5801	19	4

The gross earnings of the year under report were Rs. 5,901 - 10 – 4 against Rs. 4,758 – 9 – 8 of the preceding year, showing an increase of Rs. 1,143 – 0 – 8. The increase was owing to a corresponding increase in the number of working prisoners. The net earnings of the jail during the year under report amounted to Rs. 4,386 – 7 – 10 against Rs. 3,098 – 14 – 8, the preceding year, showing an increase of Rs. 1,287 – 9 – 2.[103]

The amount remitted to the Treasury during the year was Rs. 4,631 – 0 – 9 against Rs. 6,647 – 13 – 9 of the previous year, showing a decrease of Rs. 2,016 – 13 – 0. A large amount of money, chiefly on account of the price of bricks sold to the *mahajans* of the bazaar, reported to remain unrealized. The *Fouzdary Ahilkar* says:[104]

> "Both myself and the jailor had been absent on leave during the last 2 months of the year and the time of officiating jailor was taken up in the brick fields. Hence the shortness of the remittances to the treasury."

Orders have been issued for the immediate realization of arrears.

The following table shows the gross and the net cost of the jail as also of each prisoner during the past and the preceding year :[105]

On account of	1883 – 84	1884 – 85
Police guard	2,566 8 0	2,566 8 0
Establishment	3,338 8 3	3,527 0 0
Feeding	6,039 14 0	6,806 9 3
Contingencies	968 1 9	503 5 6
Clothing and bedding	813 3 6	927 13 0
Jail buildings and repairs	464 7 8	256 2 3
Gross cost	14,240 11 2	14,587 7 0
Deduct earnings &c	4,758 9 8	5,901 10 4
Net cost	9,482 1 6	8,685 12 8

The gross cost of the jail during the past year has increased by Rs. 346 – 11 – 10 and the net cost has decreased by Rs. 796 – 4 -10. The statement given below compares the details of the gross cost of each prisoner in the jail during the year under report with those of the preceding year.[106]

	YEARS	
	1883 – 84	1884 – 85
Jail guard	Rs. 15 7 4	14 8 0
Establishment	Rs. 20 1 9	19 14 9
Diet	Rs. 36 11 6	38 7 3
Clothing and bedding	Rs. 4 14 4	5 3 10
Buildings and repairs	Rs. 2 12 9	1 7 1
Medicines and contingencies	Rs. 5 13 3	2 13 6

The slight increase of Rs. 1 -11 - 9 per head in the cost for feeding the prisoners that from Rs. 36 – 11 - 6 of the preceding year to Rs. 38 – 7 – 3 of the year under report, owing to the rise in the price of rice during 9 months of the year.[107]

The solitary cell was completed during the year. Six men were sentenced to undergo solitary confinement.

The number of reconvicted prisoners admitted into the sudder jail was 6 only during the last year. The average period of detention of prisoners pending trial was 31 days. The general conduct of prisoners has not been on the whole so good during the year as in previous years. Five prisoners were flogged and 1 lost marks, against 4 flogged, 3 lost marks in the previous year. Four prisoners had to be put in irons for misconduct. Two new blankets and one pillow, stuffed with straw were given to each prisoner during the year. The prisoner's in a body refused to take their evening meal. Three of the ring leaders were flogged warders were ordered to lose 3 months marks each and the ordinary prisoners lost marks for two months each.[108]

During the year under report 28 prisoners were released under the rules of the mark system against 17 of the previous year. The details were given below:[109]

No	Names of persons	Offences	Term of imprisonment			Period remitted under the mark system	Date of release
			YEAR	MONTH	DAY	9 weeks	April 19th 1884
1	Jonakoo Das	395 I.P.C.	10			4 weeks	April 24th 1884
2	[illegible] Nashya	326 I.P.C.	3	-----	----	10 weeks	May 5th 1884
3	Bhelong Majhi	312 I.P.C.	3			7 weeks	June 19th 1884
4	Shahar Nashya	403 I.P.C.	2	-----	----	10 weeks	July 3rd, 1884
5	Andaroo Das	395 I.P.C.	3	-----	----	10 weeks	Do
6	Mungloo Das	DO	3	-----	----	10 weeks	Do
7	[illegible] Das	DO	3	-----	----	10 weeks	Do
8	Jugganath Das	DO	3	-----	----	11 weeks	August, 2nd, 1884
9	[illegible]	411 I.P.C.	3	-----	----	10 weeks	August 9th, 1884
10	Doyal Nashya	380 I.P.C.	3			6 weeks	July 31st, 1884
11	[illegible] Chand	498 I.P.C.	2	-----	----	5 weeks	August 1st, 1884
12	Notoroo Julloo	380 & 224 I.P.C.	1	6		7 weeks	August 30th, 1884
13	Luckhie Nashya	407 I.P.C.	3	-----	----	12 w, 2d.	Oct. 10th, 1884
14	Monie Das	395 & 224 I.P.C.	3	4	----	1 m, 26 d.	Nov. 17th, 1884
15	Notibolla	380 & 457 I.P.C.	2	4		1 m, 16 d.	Dec. 5th, 1884
16	Rupa Das	457 I.P.C.	2	-----	----	1 m, 14 d.	Dec 6th, 1884
17	Ramprasad Das	457 I.P.C.	2			Do	Do
18	Madan Das	DO	2	-----	----	Do	Do
19	Holla Das	DO	2	-----	----	Do	Do
20	Doma Shing	323 I.P.C.	5	-----	----	2 m. 5 d.	Dec. 13th, 1884
21	[illegible]	457 I.P.C.	2	6	----	19 days	Dec 27th, 1884
22	Lepra das	376 & 497 I.P.C.	5			1 m., 15 d.	Dec. 20th, 1884
23	Dukali Das	457 I.P.C.	2	7	----	1 m, 25 d	Jan 24th, 1885
24	Tonga Das	365, 366 I.P.C.	3	-----	----	5 m, 26 d.	Feb 21st, 1885
25	Rupesbur Das	407 I.P.C.	5	-----	----	4 m, 15 d.	Feb 2nd, 1885
26	Gourkant Das	497 I.P.C.	2	3		1 m, 22 d.	Feb 28th, 1885
27	Hegoora Nashya	300 I.P.C.	2	-----	----	1 m, 1 day	March 13th 1885
28	Boodharoo Nashya	457 I.P.C.	2	-----	----	1 m, 14 d.	March 10th 1885

Generally speaking, the jail officers, together with the Police guard in charge of the jail, have done their duty satisfactory. There have been no escapes during the year1885, under report although the number of prisoners was greater than those in the previous year. The number of prisoners admitted in the three lock –ups of Dinhata, Mathabhanga and Mekhligunj. During the year under report was 544 against 461 of the previous year, showing an increase of 83 prisoners.[110] The number of admissions, 544 added to 41 the number that remained in the lock – ups at thc cnd of the previous year, gives a total of 585. Out of this 157 were transferred to the Sudder jail, 397 released, 2 escaped and 29 remitted in the lock –ups at the end of the year. The cost per head of the prisoners in the lock ups amounted to Rs. 35 – 10 -3, against Rs. 35 – 1 - 10 in the previous year showing a slight increase of Rs. 0 – 8 – 5 per head. The attention of the sub – divisional officers was drawn to the subject of reducing expenditure on this head by the *Fouzdary Ahilkar* and this officer remarks:[111]

> "I am glad that the sub–divisional officer of Mathabhanga, has acted up to my suggestion and has been able to show a reduction of about Rs. 4 pcr head in the cost of diet. The Naib Ahilkar states in his annual report as follows. The charge of diet of each prisoner during the year was Rs. 40 – 1 - 5 against Rs. 44 – 7 – 9 of the previous year. This decrease was owing to fuel which were formally

> supplied by the Mathabhanga shop keepers but jungle trees are brought from waste lands for fuel."

There were two escapes during the year one from Dinhata and the other from the Mathabhanga lock – up. The *Naib – Ahilkar* attributes both the escapes to the unsatisfactory state of the buildings and the fence enclosing the yard.[112]

The *Fouzdary Ahilkar* makes the following remarks on this point :[113]

> "The expediency of appointing a warder in each of the 3 sub – divisional Lock – ups has been pointed out in the last year's report. The *Naib Ahilkar's* are of opinion that the arrangement will more than pay the expenditure that will be incurred. At present there is none to look after the prisoners outside the Lock –up *chekwar* and consequently the convicts have to spend much of their time in idleness. A kitchen –garden, close to the jail would be much profitable and immensely useful; but this cannot be done so long as there was no warder to look after the prisoners. The Mathabhnaga *Naib Ahilkar* complains of the insufficiency of the Lock –up guard. I to be regular unless the required number of constables on guard duty be weekly or fortnightly set apart, otherwise when the

> pressure of station works increases, the number of men engaged in guard duty falls short and constables who are engaged in such duty are forced to stand on guard 4 or 5 hours continuously."

The following statement shows the sickness and mortality as compared with daily strength for the past two years :[114]

YEAR	Average daily strength	PERCENTAGE OF STRENGTH			REMARKS
		Admissions	Deaths	Daily sick	
1885 – 86	160.56	107.70	4.55	4.10	
1884 – 85	177.71	123.77	3.57	3.43	

The total number of deaths were 7 viz, remittent fever 4, phthisis 1 diarrhea 1 and debility & old age 1. The healthiest month was June and December 1885, January and February 1886; daily average sick per cent of strength being in these months 3.7, 3.5, 1.42 and 1.47 respectively. The unhealthiest months were April, May, August and September 1885; daily average sick percent being in these months 5.50, 6.0, 5.20 and 5.0 respectively.[115]

The following table gives the sickness and mortality for the past two years:[116]

YEAR	POLICE				MILITARY			
	Daily average strength	PERCENTAGE OF STRENGTH			Daily Average strength	PERCENTAGE OF STRENGTH		
		Admissions	Deaths	Daily sick		Admissions	Deaths	Daily sick
1885-85	308.7	70.8	....	2.0	155.0	170.0	1.30	3.88
1884-85	309.1	97.50	......	2.50	156.1	150.25	......	4.16

The total number of State Police and military treated was 483 including 10 remaining from the previous year of which 315 suffered with malarias fever, ague and remittent and the other most prevalent disease were rheumatism, respiratory affections, dysentery and diarrhea. Among the military there was one case of cholera in April and another in June, one of which terminated fatally, also a case of remittent fever; n o deaths among the State police.[117]

In 1886–87 the general health of the jail as reported to have been remarkably good, only 3 deaths having taken place, one of which occurred in the case of a man who was suffering from advanced heart -disease at the time of admission and he was not permitted to do hard work. He fell dead one day while coming to the Hospital.[118]

The following table shows the sickness and mortality in the jail as compared with the daily strength for the last year :[119]

Description	1886–87	1887–88
1. Average population of the sudder jail	143.40	122.56
2. Admission on account of sickness	140.00	225
3. Average sick	4.20	5.37
4. Percentage of admissions to population	97.62	181.13
5. Average sick per cent of average population	2.02	4.38
6. Deaths	4.00	3
7. Death rate of 100 prisoners	2.85	2.44

The following statement shows the sickness and mortality of the past two years:[120]

YEAR	POLICE				MILITARY			
	Daily average strength	PERCENTAGE OF STRENGTH			Daily Average strength	PERCENTAGE OF STRENGTH		
		Admissions	Deaths	Daily sick		Admissions	Deaths	Daily sick
1887-88	321.2	69.73	0.64	2.50	163	130.67	0.61	3.90
1888-89	307	86.92	0.32	3.05	164	140.85	-----	4.90

The Superintendent of the State made the following remarks in 1889 :[121]

> "I am very pleased to be able to report most favourably of the general heath of the jail population throughout the year. Out of the total daily average population of 106.94 the total daily average of sickness was 4.43. the total number of admission to hospital during the year was 194."

The following table shows the sickness and mortality in the jail as a compared with the daily strength for the last two years:[122]

Description	1887–88	1888–89
1. average population of the sudder jail	122.56	106.94
2. Admission on account of sickness ——	225.0	194.00
3. Average sick ——	5.37	4.43
4. Percentage of admission to population	181.13	181.30
5. Average sick per cent of average population	4.38	4.04
6. Death ——	3	——
7. Date rate of 100 prisoners ——	2.44	——

Superintendent of the State remarks that "I would specially draw attention to the fact that not a single death during the year. I believe this is a record which has never been beaten by any Bengal jail, if indeed has by any jail in India. I attribute this excellent result due to three things viz;

1st, That the prisoners are housed in a manner more natural to them than the *pucca* buildings of Government jails.

2nd; That they are allowed a small quantity of meat or fish twice a week.

3rd; That their drinking water is now obtained from a well which is secured against contamination and the water is boiled and filtered before use.

This well water was not used during the whole year as will be noted later on. On the 22nd February Surgeon – General with the Government of India visited the jail and expressed his pleasure and approval with the state and clearness of the jail generally and of the good health enjoyed by the prisoners.

The sanitary condition of the jail was good one. The dry earth system used for night – soil, which has been buried in trenches at from about 80 to 100 yards from the jail walls.

I have however occasionally, noticed the smell from the trenches while inside the jail and on mentioning Sir B. Simpson and expressing my opinion that the trench system did not work satisfactorily owing to the dampness of the soil, he said that the trenches were too near to the jail walls.

For this reason and because there is no other land much more suitable which can be taken up for the purpose and also because the night –soil is not used as manure and the trench system therefore valueless for this purpose, I have advised that an arrangement be made by which the night–soil may be daily removed to a distance and buried along with the rest of the night – soil of the town. This will shortly be done.

The *pucca* well which I had advised last year was finished and the water commenced to be used on the 31st August 1888. It then seemed very good water. During my absence in England it became thick and was condemned on November 2nd, by the Assistant Surgeon then acting for me, who advocated the use of the water in the jail tank for drinking purpose and also discontinued the use of the filters. On my return I ordered the filters to be resumed and the water from Sagar dighi given another trial, that being better as shown by an examination than the water of the jail tank.

The well having been pumped up well out, as recommended by Sir B. Simpson, the water became clearer and a subsequent examination proved it to be perfectly good. This water, previously boiled and filtered, is now used in the jail and is most satisfactory.

At my suggestion a *pucca* bathing platform has been constructed and the drains at the back of the cook–houses have been abolished, *pucca* sinks being substituted, which are cleared by twice a day.

I have examined the food of the prisoners almost daily and have found it as before excellent in quality and ample in quantity."[123]

The following statement shows the sickness and mortality for the past two years :[124]

YEAR	POLICE				MILITARY			
	Daily average strength	PERCENTAGE OF STRENGTH			Daily Average strength	PERCENTAGE OF STRENGTH		
		Admissions	Deaths	Daily sick		Admissions	Deaths	Daily sick
1888-89	310.5	30.63	-------	2.85	165	209.20	-------	4.85
1887-88	311.2	59.73	0.54	2.50	165	130.67	0.61	3.90

In 1890–91 the general health of the jail population has been fair, though not a good as in the previous years. The Hospital Ward, which was much smaller than the original one, said to have been times inconveniently crowded at times, there being occasionally 13, 14 or 15 patients. The building was only a temporary character and this defect will be remedied in the future.[125]

One death occurred on the 4th of August from pneumonia. This was the first death that has occurred in the jail since the 15th of December 1887.[126]

The following table shows the sickness and mortality of the jail as compared with the daily population, for the last two years:[127]

Description	1889–90	1890–91
1. Average population of the sudder jail	108.63	107.02
2. Admission on account of sickness ———	234.0	290.0
3. Average sick ———	5.84	7.49
4. Percentage of admissions to population	215.41	270.97
5. Average sick per cent of average population	5.37	6.99
6. Deaths ———	——	1
7. Death rate of 100 prisoners ———	——	.09

Between 27th September and the 1st October four cases of ophthalmic occurred. This disease was epidemic at the time, there being a large number of cases in the adjacent College boarding and police hospital. The four cases in the jail were segregated and the disease did not spread beyond them.[128]

No cases of cholera occurred during the year, which the Civil Surgeon considers to be a matter for great satisfaction, as the disease was raging in an epidemic form all round.

Special precautions were taken to ward off the disease. Disinfectants were used freely and tar and sulphur were kept burning both outside and inside the jail walls. On the 18th march Dr. Hendley recommended that Prisoners working outside the jail should be prevented from drinking water from an tanks or *nullahs*, &c., and on the 19th March he further recommended that no prisoners should be sent to work at the Nilkuti at the disease was very prevalent there at the time. It is due to these wise precautions that cholera never obtained a footing in the jail, though later on two cases of severe diarrhea occurred both of which recovered.[129]

Dr. Hendely remarks regarding night – soil, drainage, food &c. :[130]

> "It is with the greatest satisfaction that I report that arrangement for the disposal of the jail night – soil came into force on the 20th December. Instead of being buried in trenches the night – soil removed in large iron

receptacles and taken to a distance and buried along with the night–soil of the town. The jail was no longer troubled with the malodorous breezes that used formerly to be wafted over it and a great source of danger has been removed. The drainage of the jail has been for the most part good, but the drains at the South East corner of the quadrangle had to be deepened once or twice, as the water collected there some-what during the rains. The drinking water and the food supplied to the prisoners continue to be excellent in quality and sufficient in quantity. I inspected both daily."

The following table shows the condition of prisoners in the jail:[131]

YEAR	POLICE				MILITARY			
	Daily average strength	PERCENTAGE OF STRENGTH			Daily Average strength	PERCENTAGE OF STRENGTH		
		Admissions	Deaths	Daily sick		Admissions	Deaths	Daily sick
1890-91	305.4	94.63	-------	7.32	188.50	144.83	1.05	7.10
1889-90	306.1	64.68	0.63	1.79	188	144.67	-----	4.04

Thus the condition of the prisoners and the system of the conduct of the jail during the rule of the Maharaja was an unique one.

NOTES AND REFERENCES

1. A.A.R. of the C.B.S (1878–79), p. 42.
2. *Ibid.*
3. *Ibid.*
4. *Ibid.*
5. *Ibid.*
6. *Ibid.*
7. *Loc.cit.*, p. 43.
8. *Ibid.*
9. *Ibid.*
10. *Ibid.*
11. *Ibid.*
12. *Ibid.*, p. 44.
13. *Ibid.*
14. *Loc.cit.*
15. *Ibid.*
16. *Ibid.*
17. *Ibid.*, p. 45.
18. *Ibid.*
19. *Loc.cit.*
20. *Ibid.*
21. *Ibid.*
22. *Ibid.*
23. A.A.R. of the C.B.S (1880–81), p. 38.
24. *Ibid.*
25. *Ibid.*
26. *Ibid.*
27. *Loc.cit.*
28. *Ibid.*
29. *Loc.cit.*
30. *Ibid.*, p. 39
31. *Ibid.*

32. *Ibid.*
33. *Ibid.*
34. *Loc.cit.*
35. *Ibid.*
36. *Ibid.*
37. *Ibid.*
38. *Ibid.*, p. 40.
39. *Ibid.*
40. *Ibid.*
41. *Ibid.*
42. *Loc.cit.*
43. *Ibid.*
44. *Ibid.*, p. 41.
45. *Ibid.*
46. *Loc.cit.*
47. *Ibid.*
48. *Ibid.*
49. *Ibid.*
50. *Ibid.*
51. *Ibid.*
52. *Ibid.*
53. *Ibid.*
54. *Ibid.*
55. A.A.R. of the C.B.C (1882–83), p. 59.
56. *Ibid.*
57. *Ibid.*, p. 60.
58. *Loc.cit.*
59. *Ibid.*
60. *Ibid.*
61. *Ibid.*
62. *Loc.cit.*
63. *Loc.cit.*

64. *Ibid.*
65. *Ibid.*
66. A.A.R. of the C.B.S (1883-84), p. 21.
67. *Ibid.*
68. *Ibid.*
69. *Ibid.* .
70. *Ibid.*
71. *Ibid.*
72. *Loc.cit.*, p. 22.
73. *Loc.cit.*
74. *Ibid.*
75. *Ibid.*
76. *Ibid.*
77. *Ibid.*
78. *Ibid.*
79. *Ibid.*
80. *Ibid.*, p. 23.
81. *Ibid.*
82. *Ibid.*
83. *Ibid.*
84. *Ibid.*
85. *Loc.cit.*, p. 24.
86. *Loc.cit.*
87. *Ibid.*
88. *Ibid.*
89. *Ibid.*, p. 15.
90. *Ibid.*
91. A.A.R. of the C.B.S. (1884–85), p. 14.

    The following are the remarks recorded by the *Fouzdari Ahilkar* in the jail visit book.

    "The usually violent storm which passed over the station this evening at about 5.30 p.m. pulled down two of the big wards of the jail. Almost all the other houses have suffered more or less. The *chekwar* of the garden has fallen down and some of the trees either broken or prostrated. As the huts cannot be removed to -night men will be employed from tomorrow to take the materials out –side the jail. Special arrangements will be made for guard to night. The mango tree, in front of the jail, to be made erect and propped up. An Earthen mound must be made at the root."

92. *Ibid.*

93. *Ibid.*

94. *Ibid.*

95. *Ibid.*

The following was the Civil surgeons account of accident :

"Prisoner Balloram Byragee under sentence of six month's imprisonment, accidentally fell into the tank yesterday at 4.50 p.m. and was drowned before the body was recovered. The man had attended the hospital in the morning and the Native Doctor exempted him from labour. I saw it last evening."

96. *Ibid.*

97. *Ibid.*, p. 15.

98. *Ibid.*

99. *Ibid.*

100. *Ibid.*

101. *Ibid.*

102. *Ibid.*

103. *Ibid.*, p. 16.

104. *Ibid.*

105. *Ibid.*

106. *Ibid.*

107. *Loc.cit.*

108. *Ibid.*

109. *Loc.cit.*, p. 17.

110. *Ibid.*

111. *Ibid.*, p. 18.
112. *Ibid.*
113. *Ibid.*
114. A.A.R. of the C.B.S. (1885–86), p. 23.
115. *Ibid.*, p. 24.

Dr. Briscoe reports :

"The sanitary condition of the jail is good, the dry earth system in the day and night privies is carried out effectually and the night soil buried out in the field; the drainage is good and there is never any lodgment of water; the food was frequently examined and always found to be of good quality, well cooked and sufficiently varied; the drinking water is brought on carts from the Sagar dighi."

116. *Ibid.*
117. *Ibid.*
118. A.A.R. of the C.B.S. (1886–87), p. 24.

The Civil Surgeon reports :

"The sanitary condition of the jail is good. The dry earth system is properly carried out but the dampness of the neighbourhood prevents the trenches outside the jail wall in which the night soil is buried, absorbing this as quickly as occurs in drier localities.

During the year I recommended the use of filters in the jail and this has been done, with great improvements to the drinking water.

I also advised that a *pucca* well should be constructed inside the jail and this has been done with great improvements to the drinking water.

I also advised that a *pucca* well should be constructed inside the jail walls for the supply of drinking water to the prisoners and this is in course of construction.

The drainage of the jail satisfactory.

The food has been inspected by me almost daily and I consider it excellent in quality and sufficient in quantity and properly varied.

Having seen the working of this jail for more than a year I am convinced of the superior healthiness of the system of housing the convicts in bamboo wards, as is done here over the *pucca* buildings such as are used in all the Government jails in Bengal."

119. *Ibid.*

120. *Ibid.*, p. 25.

121. A.A.R. of the C.B.S. (1888–89), pp. 24–25.

122. *Ibid.*

123. *Ibid.*

124. *Ibid.*

125. A.A.R. of the C.B.S. (1890–91), p. 57.

126. *Ibid.*

127. *Ibid.*

128. *Ibid.*, p. 58.

129. *Ibid.*

130. *Ibid.*

131. *Ibid.*

Conclusion

During the rule of Maharaja Harendra Narayan (1783–1839), the whole administration was under the British Commissioner, who conducted the affairs of the State in the name and on behalf of the Maharaja. He constituted in himself the highest court of appeal in all matters, whether Civil, Criminal or Revenue.

When the Maharaja assumed charge of his State after the attainment of his maturity in 1801, the administration again fell solely into the hands of the State officers, an appeal lying to the Maharaja from their decisions. The principal departments of the administration were the department of the Dewan, those of Civil and Criminal administration and the department of accounts. The Maharaja had his own office of the Munshi or Personal Assistant. The Khangi formed a branch of the Revenue department, being concerned with the management of the Maharaja's private estates.[1]

The Civil and the Criminal courts were divided into Original and Appellate and the title of the Presiding officer of the former was Ahilkar.[2]

In 1803, the Government determined to introduce in Cooch Behar the system of law or Provinces and to place the Courts under its own officers; but owing to the strenuous opposition made to this measure by the Maharaja, it was abandoned and the Government contented itself with remodeling the courts of the country under native officers.[3]

When Mr. Macleod was appointed Commissioner in 1813 the Government had in view the reconstruction of the Courts of the State and the organization of an efficient Police. The Government drew out a scheme for the purpose and asked the Commissioner to obtain the assent of the Maharaja to its introduction. But it does not appear that the measure was adopted in the country during the life – time of the Maharaja.[4]

The law administered was the Hindu law, both in matters Civil and Criminal and there was one law one law both for Hindus and Mahamedans. There were Pandits attached to the courts to expound the law.[5]

Under the Maharaja's authority death by hanging was the penalty infected on special criminals.[6]

The British Commissioners had a separate office of their own and their own Dewans.[7]

The want of a regular organized system of Police was one of the chief defects of the administration and like the system of Land Revenue was sadly in want of reform. Ever since the State came into contact with the English, one of the earliest endeavors of Government had been to organize an efficient system of Police in the State. Gang robberies and public offences used to be committed along the Rangpur frontier with perfect impunity, as the offenders on being pursued sought in Cooch Behar and applications to the State for assistance uniformly failed of success.[8]

During the minority of the Maharaja the British Commissioners did something to improve the condition of the Police in the country. In 1805 there were two Thanas in the State, one at Atharabenki, south of Dinhata and the other at Mekhligunj.[9] These had evidently been established by Mr. Ahmuty. In the following year a third was established near Balarampur and was probably the Bhabanigunj Thana, in place of which Tufangunj sprang up in subsequent years.[10]

The interference, which the Government was obliged to make in the administration of the country even after the Maharaja had come of age was for the most part necessitated by the want of an efficient Police in the State and the consequent insecurity it occasioned to the neighboring district of Rangpur. One of the missions of the Commissioners' since appointed was thus the reform of Police and the organization of a proper system of checking and detecting crimes. But the good endeavors' of the Commissioners in this respect always met with failure, owing to the Maharaja's strong repugnance to British reform. The result was that crimes went unchecked and the country did not enjoy that security of person and property which so prominently marks the present administration of the State.[11]

In 1836, the Government ruled that persons accused of heinous crimes and absconding from British India into Cooch Behar and vice versa should be demanded from or given up to the authorities of that principality and that the practice should be strictly reciprocal.[12]

Maharaja Harendra Narayan appears to have been authorized by the express permission of Government to retain in his service a company of sepoys numbering 120 men as a personal guard and a body of 150 Burkundazes to be employed in the collection of his revenue and the discharge of other current duties under his revenue and the discharge of other current duties under his government.[13] In 1814 the Maharaja in addition to these employed 5 companies of rabble sepoys, comprising altogether 335 men and a body of 171 Burkundazs. The time was very unsettled and Bhutia aggressions were constantly taking place. The new enlistment was thus a necessity. The Commissioner, however, took a different view and asked the Government to require the Maharaja to discharge all the additional sepoys and Burkandazs, which was according done. Only eight of the new batch of Burkundazes were kept on to act as a guard at Maraghat to repel the incursions of the Bhutias.[14]

In 1816, Commissioner Mr. MacLeod made a proposal of further reducing the force, but this was not sanctioned by the Government.[15]

In 1833, the Maharaja purchased from Government 180 muskets for his own use. On this occasion the Government presented him with two six–pounder brass guns.[16]

The Sepoy, as already noticed, served as a personal guard of the Maharaja. Small guards were often stationed at places near the frontiers where the disturbance was great. Thus there were gurads at Maraghat, Ksheti, Pundibari and Berbera in Jaldhoya. From time to time companies of Government sepoys had also to be posted to Cooch Behar to prevent disturbances at the frontiers.[17]

The State of Sepoys were without discipline and generally useless for active service. Proper control was not kept over them and they were sometimes found to extort money from the villagers and occasionally take part in dacoities within the State. They were not regularly paid. Their degeneration was thus inevitable.[18]

Regarding the administration of the State a brief note can be made on the basis of the following points. In broad lines of the British Administration of the State during the minority of the Maharaja and the general principles of government adopted by His Highness after his installation have already appeared. The details of both were as follows :[19]

In the Memorandum of Administration the following broad lines of Government were laid down:

1. The position hitherto occupied by the British Government regarding the State was assumed by His Highness.
2. Functions of the Commissioner were in a general way delegated to the State Council and those of the Deputy Commissioner, divided among three officers, viz, the Superintendent of the State, the Dewan and the Civil Judge.

Three degrees of authority were thus created in the country; First, His Highness, the Ruler of the State and Supreme Head of the Government; secondly the State Council, the main deliberative and controlling body and immediate head of the Judiciary and the Executive and thirdly; the Departmental Heads, the actual workers of the administration.

The Council was opened with His Highness as President and three members namely the Superintendent of the State, who was the ex-officio Vice – President, The Dewan, who was the senior member and the manager of the Chaklarjat Estates. No one had yet been appointed to the newly created post of the Civil Judge. The Judicial Member first took seat in the Council on the 2nd February 1884.[20]

Lieutenant Colonel A. Evans Gordon I.S.E. was the first Vice President of the Council and Superintendent of the State and joined his office in November 1883. He was an Officer lent by Government and reverted to Government service on the 31st October 1891. Rai Calica Doss Dutt Bahadur, C.I.E., Senior member of the Council and Dewan of the State acted in both the capacities in addition to his own duties so long as Mr. E.E. Lewis, a late Commissioner of the Rajshahi Division and Political agent for the State, who was appointed as Lieutenant-Colonel Gordon's successor in Office, did not relieve him on the 3rd December of that year. Mr. Lewis was succeeded by Mr. D. R. Lyall, C.S.I., late Member of the Revenue Board, Bengal on the 2nd April 1896. His term of Office expired in March 1899 and he was succeeded by Major J.R.C. Colvin, I.S.C., the present Vice–President of the Council, and Superintendent of the State. The services of this officer have been lent by Government.[21]

Rai Calica Doss Dutt Bahadur, C.I.E, likewise an Officer lent by Government, who had been the Dewan since 1869, was appointed Senior Member of the state Council after the institution. He has since been holding both the offices. On his retirement from Government service in 1893 -94, his services were specially retained by His Highness.[22]

Rai Balaram Mallick Bahadur, B.L., a Subordinate Judge of Bengal, whose services were lent to the State by Government was appointed Judicial Member of the Council and Civil Judge and took over charge of his duties on the 31st January 1883. On his reversion to Government service in December 1886, Babu Jadub Chandra Chakravarti, an officer lent by Government, who had been the *Fauzdari Ahilkar* of his duties on the 31st December. He retired from service on the 1st August 1898 and was succeeded by Babu

Priyanath Dutta, M.A., B.L., the Present incumbent, on promotion from the post of the *Fauzdari Ahilkar.*[23]

The President has, in all deliberations of Council, the casting vote, the other Members having single votes. Three Members form a quorum. During the temporary vacancy in the post of any member, the *Fouzdati Ahilkar* is general authorized to sit in the Council to form the quorum.[24]

On all past occasions when His Highness was away from India, the Councilors were authorized by him by special memoranda to carry on the administration with almost supreme powers during his absence.[25]

The first meeting of the State Council was held on the 12th November 1883.

The functions of the State Council were three–fold: Legislative, Executive and Judicial. On the Legislative side the Council passes laws and enactments. On the Executive side it regulates the management of the different departments. In matters Judicial the Council was the highest Court of Appeal, having final jurisdiction in Civil, Criminal and Revenue suits and proceedings. The Council have the power to frame rules and regulations for the management of the judicial side.[26]

As already noticed, the departments under the control of the State Council of the State Council are three in number, namely, the General Department, the Revenue Department and the Civil or judicial Department. The Superintendent of the State was the Head of the first, the *Dewan* of the second and the Civil and Sessions Judge of the third. The different subordinate branches of the administration under each of the Departmental Heads were noted below :[27]

General Department : 1. Administration of Criminal Justice; 2. Police; 3. Jail and Lock-ups; 4. Education; 5. Public Works; 6. Agriculture and Forest; 7. Medical; 8. Military; 9. Philkhana; 10. State Press; 11. State Library; *Rcvcnue Department*: 1. Land Revenue; 2. Settlement; 3. Treasury and Stamp Revenue; 4. Excise Revenue; 5. Offices at the Rajbari; *Judicial Department*: 1. Civil and Criminal Justice; 2. Registration.

Under the head of the general Department were shortly noticed : 1. Criminal Justice - Police – Jail - Lock –up; 2. Public Works; 3. Medical; 4. Education and 5. Miscellaneous.

1. Criminal Justice and Police and Jail and Lock–up :[28]

Mr. Smith, Deputy Commissioner, has the following in his Annual Report for 1872 -73 regarding the history and constitution of the Criminal courts in the State :

> "It seems probable that justice was dispensed by the Raja or his minister in primitive fashion as late as late as 1791; for when Mr. Douglas, Commissioner, took charge of Cooch Behar in that year he took the administration of Civil and Criminal Justice in his own hands. The Civil

> and Criminal Courts of original jurisdiction namely the court of the *Dewani Ahilkar* and that of the *Fouzdari Ahilkar*, appear to have been constituted when the British authorities withdrew from interference in the internal affairs of Cooch Behar and were doubtless in imitation of the *Muffusil* courts of the East India Company. Hindu law was referred to in both Civil and Criminal cases but the regulations naturally had a powerful influence, being the only modern laws known to the Bengali *amla* who administered the affairs of the Raj.

When the Commissioner took charge of Cooch Behar on behalf of the Raja in 1864, the Criminal Courts existing were, first, the Raj–Sabha in which the Raja or the Sarvarahakar, assisted by the two *Dewans*, disposed of appeals from the Court of Sessions; Secondly; the Court of Sessions which tried heinous offenders and heard appeals from the *Fauzdari Ahilkar*. This Court professed to be guided by the Shastras but the Pandits, while advising the Judge of the Sentence Prescribed by the Sastras, used to suggest some other punishment more consonant with modern ideas and the Judge was at liberty to disregard both the Pandits suggestion and the doctrine of the Hindu Code. Thirdly, the Court of the *Fouzdari Ahilkar* and that of his Assistant, who were guided not by Hindu Law, but by the spirit of the Regulations.

During 1864 and 1865, the time of the Commissioner being monopolized by a great extent by the Bhutan expedition, no extensive changes were made in the Administration of Criminal Justice. The work of the Raj–Sabha was transferred to the Commissioner's Office. The Constitution and procedure of the Sessions Court were retained, a former Session Judge, a native was reinstated and two additional *Naib Ahilkars* were appointed to clear off the accumulated arrears of the *Fouzdari* Court.

In 1866, the Indian Penal Code and the Code of Criminal Procedure were introduced by an order of the Offg. Commissioner; the details of the Office work and procedure were revised and corrected; the native Session Judge was removed; the duties of the Civil and Session judge were added on to those of the Deputy Commissioner; the old *Fauzdari Ahilkar* was pensioned off and replaced by a more competent man and a greatly improved state of things began.

The Sub–division of the State was established at Tufangunj on the 3rd March 1866 and placed in charge of the Assistant *Fouzdari Ahilkar*. The Head –quarters of the Sub – division were in the following year removed to Dinhata " which" to quote Mr. Smith, " is a pleasanter and healthier place and situated in a more populous part of the state.

The First Sub–divisional officer had only Criminal jurisdiction; in 1868, owing to accumulation of work both in the Civil and Criminal departments, a second *Naib Ahilkar* was re-appointed; who exercised both Civil and Criminal powers. With the introduction of the *Khas* collection system in the Revenue Department and establishment of four additional sub–divisions were vested with Civil and Criminal powers within their respective jurisdictions. In the following year two of the new Sub–divisions namely; LalBazar and Tufangunj were abolished and the Muffusil Criminal Courts were brought down to three."

The powers of the Sessions Judge formerly extended to passing a sentence of 14 years imprisonment; cases requiring heavier punishment were formerly referred to the Raj – Sabha and subsequently to the Commissioner.[29] Capital punishment had not been inflicted for many years before the Commissioner took charge in 1864. The Sessions cases were tried with the assistance of a Law – Officer or with assessors. The Law–Officer was Pandit Bikramananda Bhattacharya of Khagrabari. The Session Court also heard appeals from the decisions of the *Fauzdari Ahilkar* and the *Naib Ahilkars*. All decisions of the *Fauzdari Ahilkar* were subject to appeal to the judge.[30]

The powers of the *Fauzdari Ahilkar* extended to two years rigorous imprisonment and a fine of Rs. 200 (Narani) commutable to one additional year's imprisonment. He had no powers to hear appeals from the subordinate Magistracy. In cases regarding punishment heavier than what the *Fauzdari Ahilkar* could inflict he committed to the Sessions. He had the charge of the Police and the Jail.[31]

Before the opening of the Sub – divisions the Assistant *Fauzdari Ahilkar* and the *Naib Ahilkar* at the Sudder had no power to receive complaints; they tried such cases as were made over to them by the *Fauzdari Ahilkar*. The powers of these Officers extended to six months imprisonment and a fine of Rs. 50.[32]

Formerly, a special or second appeal lay from the appellate decision of the Sessions Judge in criminal cases to the Commissioner. The practice was abolished in 1868. In that year all sentences of imprisonment not exceeding one month or of fines not exceeding Rs. 50, passed by the *Fauzdari Ahilkar*, were made final and not subject to appeal.[33]

The Indian Criminal Procedure Code of 1872 (Act X of 1872) was introduced in the State in September 1873. On the introduction of that Code the practice and procedure of Criminal Courts came to be guide by that enactment with certain modifications. The Sub – divisional officers had the powers of Subordinate Magistrates of the first class under the code, but had no jurisdiction in proceedings under the Code.[34] In 1875 the Sub–divisional *Naib Ahilkars* were empowered to require security for good behavior in cases under section 504 of the Criminal Procedure Code. In the following year their jurisdiction was extended to the kidnapping cases. Cases of adultery were not formerly cognizable by them as at present.[35]

Besides the powers under the Criminal procedure Code the *Fauzdari Ahilkar* all along enjoyed a summary jurisdiction cases for the recovery of wife. On an application from the husband the absconding wife was brought up on a warrant and was if she admitted marriage, made over to the husband; when marriage was denied the husband was referred to the Civil Court.[36]

The Bengal Cattle Trespass Act (Act III of 1857) was acted up to in the State from a very early time. Subsequently the spirit of Act I of 1871 was followed.[37]

In 1850, the Raj –Sabha had prohibited gambling. The spirit of the Gambling Act (Act II of 1867 B.C.), was ordered to be followed in the Courts of the State in June 1870.[38]

The custom of boring the skin and riding the Charak – pole on the Chait sankranti day was prohibited in July 1871.[39]

The Indian Evidence Act (Act I of 1872) was introduced in Cooch Behar in May 1873. Before that time Norton's Law of Evidence used to be followed in the trials before Magistrates.[40]

Although the Postal Act was not introduced the Cooch Behar Courts were declared competent to take cognizance of Postal offences in December 1874.[41]

Formerly, no diary of witnesses in criminal cases was kept. In January 1866, the system of keeping a register of the examination of witnesses was introduced. Before the introduction of the Criminal Procedure Code the witnesses received no diet – money, not even in Sessions cases.[42]

The Magistrate's power to inflict whipping was regulated by Act VI of 1864, although that law was never formally introduced in the State. Similarly, there was no Oaths Act in force, although oaths were administered under the spirit of the Government Act.[43]

Formerly, the Rajgans or the kinsmen of the Maharaja, do not appear to have been subject to the jurisdiction of the Criminal Courts of the State. In August 1871, owing to a disorderly behavior of a principal Rajgan Colonel Haughton extended the jurisdiction of the Deputy Commissioner to the trial of offences committed by a Rajgan under certain restrictions.[44]

In 1892 – 93, the jurisdiction of the Fauzdari Ahilkar was extended to the trial of "summons cases" against the Rajguns. Five years later, in 1897 – 98, this privilege of the Rajgans was withdrawn and His Highness was pleased to order that in criminal cases no distinction should in future be made between Rajgans and other persons.[45]

The heavy crimes common in Cooch Behar of old days were deceits and burglary. They were no doubt attributable to the absence of an organized system of Police in the State and the consequent facility with which the offenders evaded justice. Another sort of complaint very frequent was the charge of seduction of the wives brought by many a husband. Murders generally had their origin in domestic intrigue and connubial infidelity. Murders for the sake of extorting or gaining property were of very rare occurrence. Lives were also very rarely lost in disputes over land or other property within the country.[46]

Mr. Smith gave some statics which were valuable, as enabling us to compare the State of Cooch Behar in his time as regards the prevalence of crime not only with its present state but also with what then existed in the neighboring district of Jalpaiguri. "The population", writes he in 1872 – 73,[47] " is not much tempted to crime by want. In some places tigers and leopards hinder thieves from roaming abroad after dark and in this respect act more efficiently than any Chaukidar. On the other hand, the absence of Zamindars who settle many petty cases in the Zillahs and the recent multiplication of the Sub – divisional Courts, tend to increase the number of criminal cases brought to light. Consequently found that the work to be performed by the Criminal Courts very considerable. The criminal work in Cooch Behar was more than double of what it was in Jalpaiguri, for in the latter district the number of Cognizable and non – cognizable cases reported in the past year including false ones was 1,018 against 2,224 in Cooch Behar. The number of persons brought to trial during the year under report has been 2,106 or 39 per cent of the population. The number of convictions gave almost exactly one criminal conviction to each square mile."

Mr. Dalton in his retrospect of the British Administration of Cooch Behar, written in the beginning of 1884 has the following on the condition of crimes in the State :[48]

> "The earliest record of the State shows of the number of dacoities in any one year was for 1865 – 66, when there were 12 cases. In 1867 – 68, there were 16 and in the following year 14. In 1869 – 70 there were seven and in 1870 – 71 five only. In the famine year of 1874 – 75 the number rose to 11.

In the following year seven dacoities occurred; but during the year a patrol system was organized and the returns for 1876 – 77 show one dacoity only. In 1881 -82, there were four dacoities; in 1882 -83, two only. And of late years very few of the dacoities reported have been committed by organized gang of dacoits. Some of them can be more technically called dacoities being house – trespass committed by five or more persons but unaccompanied by any serious attempt at violence. Of serious offences against the person, cases of rape, kidnapping and adultery were the most common.

Most of the murders which take place in Cooch Behar have their origin in domestic intrigue or connubial infidelity. It was very rare that murder and robbery were found in conjunction.

In short there was a very little heavy crime in the State though it compared so unfavorably with Jalpaiguri when Mr. Smith wrote his report in 1873. The total number of cases of all descriptions which occurred in 1882 – 83 approximate in a singular manner to the number reported exactly 10 years previous, the figures, being 2,224 for the former year and 2,244 for the later. Considering the increase in population and in the wealth of the people the result is most satisfactory, for while it is quite certain that the number of petty crimes, which are brought to notice must have increased considerably that fact in itself proves that serious crime has been effectively repressed."

After the Installation heavy crime gradually decreased. During the first five years, from 1883–84 to 1887–88, the number of dacoities was 18; in the next quinquonnial period it came down to 14; and in the following period ending with 1897-98, it further decreased and stood at 11. Under the Police organization scheme the bordering out – posts were abolished in that year. In the next two years alone 10 dacoities occurred, the number in 1899 – 1900, namely eight for exceeding that in any single previous year.[49]

The total number of cases of all descriptions ranged between 2,000 and 4,000 a year from 1883–84 to 1887–88, between 2,300 and 2,800 from 1888–89 to 1892–93; and between 2,000 and 2,500 during the next quinquennial period. In 1898-99, it came up to 2500 and in the following year, to 2,575. The number of cases has not thus on the whole much increased.[50]

One of the most important missions of the old Commissioners was the reform of the Police of the State. Owing to the opposition of Maharaja Harendranarayan this object could not be carried out satisfactory by any of them, although Mr. Ahmuty established two Thanas in the interior.

The State of the Police was all along an opprobrium of Cooch Behar. The pay of the Daroga was only Rs. 7 – 8 a month and a Burkundaz had to get only Rs. 2 – 4; and the whole cost of the Police establishment did not exceed Rs. 8,000 a year. Even these pittances were often not paid; for the old rule in Cooch Behar was that the Magistrate and his subordinates received no pay fines and institution fees.[51] If there was a surplus it was paid into the Majudat or Reserve Treasury; and if there was a deficiency the establishments were not paid. This system, strange as it was, worked very disastrously on the appellate Court, where there very few fines or fees and as a consequence the pay of its establishment was sometimes 12 or 13 years in arrears. In 1864, Colonel Haughton initiated the reform by appointing a Daroga for the Kotwali on Rs. 100 per month.[52]

The new Police was established in 1866 by Colonel Bruce captain Hedayat Ali was for some time in charge of the Police. In February that year Maulvie Anwarooj Zaman, an Inspector from the Bengal constabulary was appointed at the head of the Cooch Behar Police. In the course of the next year the organization of the new Police was in full force and appears to have been completed by the end of the year 1866–67.[53]

The new force was composed of 1 Superintendent, 3 Inspectors, 8 Sub–Inspectors, 26 Head Constables and 200 Constables. Excepting the Superintendent and the Inspectors, the pay of all ranks was the same as in the Bengal Police and the cost was about Rs. 40,000 a year. The force was gradually strengthened by the addition of 3 Sub – Inspectors, 1 Head – Constable and 4 constables till 1873 – 74, from the beginning of which, However, considerable reductions were made, so that at the end of the year the strength stood at 1 Superintendent, 2 Inspectors, 6 Sub – Inspectors, 21 Head – Constables and 195 Constables and the total cost of the department amounted to Rs. 32,000.[54]

The consequence of this reduction was disastrous. For want of a sufficient number of Head – Constables, ordinary constables had to be employed in the investigation of important cases; almost all privilege leave had to be stopped, which created discontent amongst the men and enabled the temporary constables to commit irregularities with impunity; and the Reserve was at so low an ebb that necessary escorts to remit treasure could not be supplied on more than one occasion. In fact the efficiency of the Police was greatly decreased.[55]

This state of affairs could not continue long. Accordingly in the following year a scheme was submitted for increasing the force and opening one new Thana and two Out – Posts, which was sanctioned with effect from 1876 – 77, when the force came to be composed of, besides the Superintendent, 3 Inspectors, 8 Sub - Inspectors, 28 Head – Constables and 240 constables. The cost came up to about Rs. 34,000.[56]

Additions and alterations in the above scale continued to be made from time to time. The post of an Assistant Superintendent was created in 1883 and at the end of 1883 – 84, the force came to be composed of 1 Superintendent, 1 Assistant Superintendent, 3 Inspectors, 10 Sub – Inspectors, 29 Head – Constables and 265 Constables and the annual cost in round number rose to about Rs. 47,000.[57]

In 1889–90, the post of the Assistant Superintendent was abolished; the grades of pay of the Inspectors were revised; and a small detective department was established. The lower rank of the police was gradually strengthened, of the police on the lines adopted in Bengal was sanctioned until in 1897 – 98 the number of constables came up to 281 and the cost of the total strength amounted to about Rs. 58,000.[58]

In that year a scheme for the reorganization of the police on the lines adopted in Bengal was sanctioned by His Highness in Council. Under that scheme the five frontier Out – posts of Kholta, Bhaishkhuchi, Sitai, Gitaldaha and Moranga were abolished resulting in the reduction of investigating centres, and the number of Head – Constables; and provision was made for the investigation of all cases by Sub – Inspectors, as far as possible and for the strengthening of the Reserve. By this the cost was slightly brought down and the strength stood as follows in 1899–1900 :[59]

Superintendent of Police	1
Inspectors	3
Sub – Inspectors	11

Head – Constables ———————— 24

Constables —————————————— 262

With an area of 1307 square miles and a population of 5,78,868 souls, the State thus has almost 1 police to every 9.5 square miles of its extent and 4,225.3 souls of its population.

The town or Municipal Police was organized in 1885 with one *Jamadar* and 23 *Chowkidars* for the town of Cooch Behar at a cost of Rs. 1,776. This has since expanded and some of the *muffasil* town, such as Haldibari, Mathabhanga and Dinhata have got it. The Municipal Police was under the Superintendent of Police.[60]

Up to the year 1875, there was nothing in the nature of a rural police of *Chowkidars* in Cooch Behar. The necessity for such a body hardly existed among the primitive people of the State who do not live in villages but in detached homesteads, over each of which the *Dewani* reigned as civil head of the community and adjusted disputes among his relatives and dependants. But with the Land Revenue settlement and the consequent greater security of hereditary rights, as people began to amass money and household property and as they became more exposed to the depredations of petty malefactors, the want of a village watch, which in Rangpur and jalpaiguri had long been established came to be more and more felt.[61] This was brought to the notice of the Deputy Commissioner in 1876 by some petitions, which began to come in from the chief inhabitants of a few *Taluks* praying for investing the *Chowkidars*, to be nominated and paid by them, with police functions and a badge as the symbol of office.[62] This prayer was granted and other *Taluks* followed suit year after year; the body increased until in 1882 – 83 there were 1,576 *chowkidars* in the State. But the novelty having worn off the men of the force were no longer able to realize their pay according to the list of subscriptions volunteered as easily as in the beginning and it was proposed to pass as Act to place the villages under a regular contribution according to the valuation of their holdings. The Cooch Behar Village *Chowkidari* Act 9 Act III of 1893) was passed in 1893 – 94. The number of *Chowkidars* in the State came up to 1,577 at the end of 1899 – 1900.[63]

In 1864, there were five *Thanas* and four Faris or Out–posts in the State as noted below :[64]

Thanas : 1. Kotwali; 2. Dinhata; 3. Mekhligunj; 4. Giladanga; 5. Bhabanigunj.

Pharis or Out – Posts — 1. Syamgunj; 2. Changrabanda; 3. Shingimari; 4. Khagrabari.

Formerly the chief point considered in connection with the site for a Police Station or Out – post was that it should be near some Bhutia stockade or village with a view to guard against Bhutia aggressions. Hence most of the out posts were put close to the Duars. As this was no longer necessary two of the stations, namely Bhabanigunj and Giladanga were removed from their old sites in 1865 – 66. Bhabanigunj, which occupied the present site of Alipur Duars, was removed to Tufangunj and Giladanga to

Mathabhanga both on the high road from Dhubri to Jalpaiguri. In 1866–67 the Out–posts of bilshi and Singimari were, owing to their unhealthy position, removed to Jamaldaha and Bhaishkhuchi, respectively. The Out – post of Khagrabari was of no use in its old place and was removed to Shitalkhuchi near the boaders of Rangpur.[65]

In the course of the next decade several Out–posts and one Thana was established so that at the end of 1876 – 77 the under mentioned Stations and Out–posts were in existence :[66]

Stations	**Out–Posts**
Kotwali	Kholta
Tufangunj	Bhaiskuchi
(afterwards called Fulbari)	Keshoribari
	Shitalkuchi
Dinhata	Ksheti (moranga)
Mathabhanga	Kotebhajni
Mekhligunj	Haldibari

After the opening of the Railway Station at Haldibari and with development of traffic, the outpost at Huldibari was converted into a Thana in 1878. The Out–post at khesoribari was removed to Shitai and two more out–posts were opened, one at Balarampore and the other at Gitaldaha, before 1885–86. The Out–post at Shitalkuchi was raised to the status of Police Station in 1893–94.[67]

In 1896–97, on the creation of the Tufangunj sub–division the Out–posts at Balarampore and

Kotebhajni were abolished to find additional force for the new sub–division.[68]

By the reorganization of the Police in 1897–98, all the remaining Out–posts have been limited to their present number, namely the five station of Kotwali, Fulbari, Dinhata, Mathabhanga and Mekhligunj and the independent Out–post of Shitalkuchi.[69]

Formerly there was no *thana* or zamindari Dak in the State. In 1864, Colonel Haughton introduced one. This was gradually replaced by the Government Postal System, which as it spread over the country, made the keeping up of a separate establishment of its own by the State quite unnecessary. The last lines of the Zamindary Dak, namely one from Cooch Behar to Bhaishkhuchi and the second from Dinhata to Shitai were abolished in 1899 and converted into Imperial lines.[70]

A Jail for the custody of prisoners had been in existence from a very old time. Formerly it was divided into two distinct departments Civil and Criminal. The Civil Jail was entirely under the *Dewani Ahilkar* and the Magistrate had no control over it. When the Commissioner took charge of the State the number of prisoners in the Civil Jail was abnormally large.[71] This was due to the old practice of bringing up the defendants on warrants on the filing of the plaint and of demanding security from them and committing them to Jail on their inability to furnish the same. In the beginning of 1866, the Commissioner required the Civil Courts to confirm to the provision of Act VIII of 1859 as much as possible and the practice of imprisoning defendants on the institution of suits was abolished.[72]

In the time of the old Maharaja the prisoners used to go out and purchase their own food from the bazaar. The ordinary prisoners received in cash one *anna* and six pictures and the life convicts two *annas* per head for the price of their ration. When Colonel Haughton came this practice was put a stop to and the convicts were fed in the jail. The scale of diet in vogue in the Bengal jails was not, however, introduced till 1867.[73]

The old Jail having fallen out of repair a new *kutcha* one was built to the south of the sagardighi in 1864. Although an improvement upon the old one, it was far from being a good jail. The situation of the jail in the middle of the town was found inconvenient and it was also most insecure. A new *kutcha* jail was accordingly built on a site to the east of the town in 1865. That was the place where jail stands at that time. The new jail was occupied in June 1866. It had a bamboo *chekar* for the outside wall.[74]

In 1874, a proposal for the building of a *pucca* wall for the Jail was sanctioned. The Deputy Commissioner was for making the buildings *pucca* before constructing a masonry wall. The idea of making the wards of masonry had, however, to be given up on sanitary grounds and only the guard–house, the office and the godown were built of masonry. A brick-wall was constructed around the Jail with prison labour; it was completed in 1879–80.[75]

A tank inside the jail was completed with jail – labour in 1869–70. This tank supplied good water to the prisoners.[76]

There was no manufactory in the jail previous to 1866. When the making of paper was introduced as a jail manufacture and a number of old criminal records were made over for the purpose. Hitherto the convicts had been employed in making roads and clearing jungles in the town, both of which were great necessities of the times.[77]

Paper making does not appear to have been a success. In subsequent yards further branches of manufacture were introduced. In subsequent years further branches of manufacture were introduced. In 1869–70 eight selected prisoners were placed in the Artizan's School to learn weaving, carpentry, pottery, smith's work, etc. A class was also opened in the Jail for teaching the convicts to read and write.[78]

> "The principal branches of manufacture", writes Mr. Dalton in 1875–76, "On which the prisoners were employed (last Year) are carpentry, twine–making, weaving, mat–making, making of bamboo chairs, *moras* and *chawkis* etc. and *sataranch*–making. The last that was *sataranch*–making was introduced in September last and it has been observed that 10 men have already mastered the work. There is also a black–smith's shop in the Jail managed by prisoners. Grinding flour,

> baking bread and working the oil – will also found employment for a number of prisoners."[79] The articles turned out by the jail were sometimes of a very good quality. Brick–making was one of the chief manufactures in the jail from 1876–77 to 1885–86. A bakery was opened in 1874 and very good bread used to be prepared in the jail. As, however, it was not paying it was stopped in April 1893. Course gunny, flour oils and articles of carpentry are the chief among the Jail manufactures of the day.[80]

A jail garden was opened in 1868 and gave employment to those prisoners who were unfit for hard labour.[81]

The mark system for the regulation of the conduct of the convicts was introduced in 1873.[82]

The Jail code of Bengal was followed in the management of the jail and Lock – ups in the State.[83]

The *Fauzdari Ahilkar* was in charge of the Jail, and was assisted by a Jailor and one Assistant Jailor.

The warders watch the prisoners when on duty, the jail was under guards supplied by the Police.[84]

The figure given below will furnish some prison statistics for the Cooch Behar Jail during the last quarter of a century:[85]

Year	No. of convicts	No. of deaths	Amount of total earning Rs	Amount of total cost Rs	Gross cost per prisoner Rs	As.	P.	Net cost per prisoner Rs.	As	P
1873–75 -----	526	18	7,443	15,224	74	15	0	43	5	2
1879–80 -----	577	21	7,883	16,582	67	3	5	57	2	2
1883–85 -----	389	7	5,021	13,842	36	8	2	64	15	4
1889–90 -----	496	----	4,157	9,055	122	5	9	83	10	6
1893–95 -----	432	2	3,002	13,803	142	4	6	105	2	9
1899–1900 ----	406	1	3,838	11,221	111	15	3	72	7	0

The figures establish three important points: First that the number of convicts has gradually but very markedly decreased; secondly that the health of the jail has been very largely improved and thirdly that the actual cost per prisoner has increased. The increase of cost per prisoner was chiefly due to the falling off in admissions.[86]

The Cooch Behar Jail was remarkable for its healthiness Sir Steuart Bayley; Lieutenant–Governor of Bengal who visited Cooch Behar in 1889 was pleased to remark "that the prisoners seemed to be well fed and properly cared for."[87]

Prisoners under transportation for life from Cooch Behar were under an arrangement with Government sent to Port Blair in the Andamans where there were maintained at the cost of the State.[88]

The first Lock–up opened in the State was at Dinhata on the transfer of the Tufangunj Sub–divisional office to that place in 1870. With the opening of the four additional Sub–divisions, the head – quarters of three of which were in the *muffusil*, the number of Lock–ups was increased from 1 to 4 in 1872. This was however, reduced to 3 in the following year with the abolition of two of the Sub – divisions. The Lock–ups thus retained in 1873, namely, those at Dinhata, Mathabhanga and Mekhligunj, do still exist. A fourth was opened at Fulbari in 1896, on the establishment of the new Tufangunj Sub–division.[89]

In the beginning there were no separate buildings for the Lock–ups and the prisoners used to be kept in the Thana buildings. Subsequently regular Lock–ups were built with the Thana guard house in their front and a high bamboo wall covering the remaining sides. The Lock–ups were built with the Thana guard house in their front and a high bamboo wall covering the remaining sides. The Lock–ups have separate cells for male and female prisoners. There was however, no accommodation for separating the under–trial prisoners from the Civil prisoners. There were no arrangements for segregation of prisoners. There were no arrangements for segregation of prisoners and no work–shop.[90]

Prisoners sentenced to 15 days imprisonment and under were confined in the Lock–ups.[91]

The number of admissions in the Lock–ups were 379 in 1873–74; which gradually rose and came up to 461 in 1883–84. Subsequently it went on decreasing till in 1895–96, the year previous to the opening of the new Tufangunj sub– division, it stood at 384. In 1897–98, the admissions in the four Lock–ups 576, but afterwards came down to 456 in 1899 – 1900.[92]

The cost of maintaining prisoners in the Lock–ups amounted to Rs. 41 – 5 – 1 per head per *annam* in 1873 – 74. It came down to Rs. 84 – 1 – 10 by 1883 – 84 but rose to Rs. 57 – 3 – 9 in 1897 – 99. The year 1899 – 1900 showed a further increase to Rs. 84 – 11 – 11. As in the case of the Jail, the falling off in admissions mostly served to raise the average cost of maintenance of the population of the Lock–ups.[93]

The Lock–ups were under the management of the Sub–divisional officers. The Sub–divisional Accountant was the ex–officio jailor and was assisted by one warder. The guard was furnished by the Police and consists of four constables under a Head–constables.[94]

Management as already noticed all these branches of the General Departments were under the immediate control of the *Fauzdari Ahilkar*, who was the District Magistrate. He was assisted in the administration of criminal Justice by the Superintendent of police and the *Naib–Ahilkars*, the latter being Executive and Judicial officers like the Deputy Magistrates of British India.[95] The *Naib Ahilkars* are in charge of the Sub–divisions and have also Civil and Revenue jurisdiction. In 1886, the last grade of the State Judicial and Executive Service was created by the appointment of Sub–*Naib Ahilkars*, whose status was that of the Sub–Deputy Magistrates and Collectors of Bengal for the assistance of the *Naib Ahilkars*. Besides the Sudder, one Sub–*Naib Ahilkar* is posted to each of the two heavy Sub–divisions of Dinhata and Mathabhanga.[96]

Babu Ramesh Chandra Chatterjee, was the *Fouzdari Ahilkar* when the British Government took charge of the State in 1864. He retired in 1865–66. After a temporary arrangement of two years, during which Moulavie Anwarooz Juman, Superintendent of Police was also in charge of the *Fauzdari Ahilkar's* Office, Babu (Rai Bahadur) Jadavebandra Chakravarti, an Officer lent by the Government, was appointed *Fauzdari Ahilkar* and joined his duties on the 1st April 1869. He continued the head of the department for a long time and "earned the confidence of the Maharaja and of the people over whom he exercised authority."[97] After his promotion to the post of the Civil Judge in 1886, Babu Priyanath Dutta, M.A. B.L., then Manager of the Chaklarjat Estates, held the post of the Fauzdari Ahilkar for above 12 years, till he was promoted to the post of the Civil and Sessions Judge on the 1st August 1898. Babu Haridas Mukherjee, M.A., B.L., was appointed to succeed him, but could not be relieved of the charge of the Chaklarjat Manager's Office until June 1900; temporary arrangements were made for the discharge of the duties of the post during the period.[98]

Regarding the history of the Superintendent of the Police force was a remarkable one. The first Superintendent of Police was Moulavi Anwarooz Jaman, an Inspector of Bengal Police, who was appointed in February 1866.[99] He was permanently succeeded by Babu Satyacharan Mukherjee, also a Police Inspector of Bengal, in December 1872. After service of 16 years he reverted to Government service in September 1888, when Mr. C.E. Briscoe held charge for a few months only.[100] Babu Parvaticharan Chukravarti, first grade Inspector was promoted to the post in December of that year and was after his death succeeded in January 1893, by Mr. C.E.Briscoe, whose services were lent by the Government of Bengal for two years. The present Superintendent Kumar Gojendranarayan Jr. M.R.A.C., took charge of Police on the 4th February 1895.[101]

Thus the whole law and order system was a sound one during the rule of the modern Maharaja's of Cooch Behar State. The modern outlook of the rulers ushered a new era in this field. As a result a unique system has been generated during the monarchical reign.[102]

NOTES AND REFERENCES

1. Chowdhury, H. N – *The Cooch Behar State and its land Revenue Settlement*, Cooch Behar State Press, Cooch Behar, 1903, p. 268.
2. *Ibid.*
3. *Ibid.*
4. *Ibid., p. 269.*
5. *Ibid.*
6. *Ibid.*
7. *Ibid.*
8. *The Cooch Behar Select Record, Vol. I, pp. 321– 324.*

   An analysis of this scheme was given below :

   (a) Hindu Law was to be administered in civil cases. The Civil Court was to be presided over by a respectable and intelligent native of the Hindu persuasion, aided by a Pandit thoroughly versed in the principles and doctrines of the Hindu Law. The Commissioner was to be invested with general unlimited control over the proceedings and decisions of the native Judge.

(b) In case of Intricacy or more than ordinary importance, no difficulty would occur in obtaining legal opinions from the Pandits or if necessary from the Maulavies of the Suddar *Dewani* Adalat of Calcutta.

(c) The Mahamedans were to be guided by Hindu Law.

(d) The Mahamedan law with the modification of it adopted in British territories should be administered in criminal cases in Cooch Behar. Petty cases were to be tried by the native criminal court, consisting of a Kazi, and a Mufti. In all cases affecting the lives of the Prisoners or involving severe punishment, the Commissioner was to be the Presiding Officer of the criminal court.

(e) No capital punishment should take place but with the knowledge and under the seal and signature of the Maharaja and that he should exercise the priviladge of remitting or mitigating punishment even when the law itself might condemn.

9. *Ibid.*, p. 270.
10. *Ibid.*
11. *Ibid.*
12. *Ibid.*
13. *Ibid.*
14. *Ibid.*
15. *Ibid.*, p. 271.
16. *Ibid.*
17. *Ibid.*
18. *Ibid.*
19. *Ibid.*, p. 300.
20. *Ibid.*
21. *Ibid.*, p. 301.

22. *Ibid.*
23. *Ibid.*
24. *Ibid.*
25. *Ibid.*
26. *Ibid.*
27. *Ibid.*, p. 302.
28. *Ibid.*, p. 303.
29. *Ibid.*
30. *Ibid.*, p. 304.
31. *Ibid.*
32. *Ibid.*, p. 305.
33. *Ibid.*
34. *Ibid.*
35. *Ibid.*
36. *Ibid.*
37. *Ibid.*
38. *Ibid.*
39. *Ibid.*, p. 306.
40. *Ibid.*
41. *Ibid.*
42. *Ibid.*
43. *Ibid.*
44. *Ibid.*
45. *Ibid.*
46. *Ibid.*
47. *Loc.cit.*, p. 307.
48. *Loc.cit.*
49. *Ibid.*, p. 308.
50. *Ibid.*
51. *Ibid.*
52. *Ibid.*
53. *Ibid.*, p. 309.

54. *Ibid.*
55. *Ibid.*
56. *Ibid.*
57. *Ibid.*
58. *Ibid.*
59. *Ibid.*, p. 310.
60. *Ibid.*
61. *Ibid.*
62. *Ibid.*
63. *Ibid.*, p. 311.
64. *Ibid.*
65. *Ibid.*
66. *Ibid.*
67. *Ibid.*, p. 312.
68. *Ibid.*
69. *Ibid.*
70. *Ibid.*
71. *Ibid.*
72. *Ibid.*
73. *Ibid.*, p. 313.
74. *Ibid.*
75. *Ibid.*
76. *Ibid.*
77. *Ibid.*
78. *Ibid.*
79. *Ibid.*
80. *Ibid.*, p. 314.
81. *Ibid.*
82. *Ibid.*
83. *Ibid.*
84. *Ibid.*
85. *Ibid.*

86. *Ibid.*

87. *Ibid.*

88. *Ibid.*

89. *Ibid.*, p. 315.

90. *Ibid.*

91. *Ibid.*

92. *Ibid.*

93. *Loc.cit.*

94. *Ibid.*

95. *Loc.cit.*

96. *Ibid.*, p. 316.

97. *Ibid.*

98. *Ibid.*

99. *Ibid.*

100. *Ibid.*

101. *Ibid.*

102. The Cooch Behar Darpan (1938), p. 53.

Bibliography

Primary Source :

a) Manuscript

1) Home Public Proceedings (Relevant Volumes).
2) Board of Revenue Proceedings (Relevant Volumes).
3) Proceedings of the Governor General – in–Council (Relevant Volumes).

b) Official Documents

1) *Annual Administration Report of the Cooch Behar State* (1862 –1950).
2) *Cooch Behar Census Report* – 1951, 1961.
3) *Cooch Behar Darpan* – 14th April, 1938.
4) *The Cooch Behar Gazette* – (1896, 1910, 1914, 1923, 1926, 1932, 1934, 1937, 1938, 1945, 1947).
5) *Cooch Behar Select Records,* Vol. – I & II, Cooch Behar State Press, 1884.

6) Hunter, W.W – *A Statistical Account of Bengal,* Vol. X, 6th ed., London.

7) Jenkins, F. – *Papers on Cooch Behar, selection from Bengal Government,* No. 5, Calcutta –1851.

8) Majumdar, Durgadas – *West Bengal District Gazeteers (Koch Bihar),* Feb., 1977.

C) Memoirs

1) Chawdhuri, Deendoyal, *Nripendra Smiriti,* Calcutta, 1915.

2) Devi, Gayatri and Ram, Santha, *The Memoirs of the Maharani of Jaipur, A Princes Remembers,* Vikas Publishing House Pvt. Ltd, New Delhi, 1982.

3) Das, Biswanath (ed.), *Autobiography of an Indian Princess – Memoirs of Maharani Sunity Devi of Cooch Behar,* Vikas Publishing House Pvt. Ltd., New Delhi, 1995.

4) Narayan, Nripendra, *Thirty Seven Years of Big game Shooting, Cooch Behar (The Duars & Assam),* Bombay, The Times Press, 1908.

Secondary Source :

a) Books (English)

Barma, Sukhbilas (ed.), *Socio - Political Movements in North Bengal - A Sub–Himalayan Tract, Vol – I & II,* Global Vision Publishing House, Delhi, 2007.

Barman, Rupkumar, *From Tribalism To State,* Abhijit Publications, Delhi, 2007.

Bhattachariya, P.K., *The Kingdom Of Kamta Koch Behar in Historical Perspective,* Ratna Publication & N.B.U, 2000.

Campbell, Arthur Claude, *Glimpses of Bengal, Vol –I,* 3 &4 Hare Street, Calcutta, 1907.

Chaudhuri, H. N., *The Cooch Behar State and its Land Revenue Settlement,* Cooch Behar State Press, Cooch Behar, 1903.

Copland, Ian, *The British Raj and The Indian Princes Paramountcy in Western India (1857–1930),* Orient Longman, Bombay, 1987.

Dasgupta, Ranajit, *Economy, Society and Politics in Bengal : Jalpaiguri, (1869–1947),* Oxford University Prees, Bombay, 1992.

Deb, Ranajit, *North Bengal at a Glance - Cooch Behar, Jalpaiguri, Darjeeling, Vol – I,* Purbouttar Prakashan, Kolkata, 2002.

Debnath, Sailen (ed.), *Social And Political Tensions In North Bengal (Since – 1947),* N.L. Publisher, Siliguri, 2007.

Debnath, Sailen, *Essays on Cultural History of North Bengal,* N.L. Publisher, Siliguri, 2008.

Fisher, Michael.H, *Indirect Rule in India – Residents and the Residency System (1764 - 1858),* Oxford University Press, 1991.

Gait, Edward, *A History of Assam,* Surjeet Publications, 4th Reprint, Delhi, 2008.

Ganguli, Karali Charan, *Final Report on the Survey and Settlement operations in the Cooch*

Behar State, (1913 – 1927), Cooch Behar State Press, Cooch Behar, 1930.

Ghoshal, S.C., *A History Of Cooch Behar* (Translation), Cooch Behar State Press, Cooch Behar, 1942.

Hunter, W.W, *The Annals of Rural Bengal*, London, 1897.

Jehangir, Sarabji, *Princes and Chiefs of India, Vol. –II*, London, 1903.

Kerr, Ian. J, *Building the Railway of the Raj (1850 – 1900)*, Oxford University Press, Delhi, 1997.

Majumdar, Prof. Amlanjyoti, *Literary Works of Maharaja Jitendra Narayan Bhup Bahadur of Cooch Behar,* N.L. Publisher, Siliguri, 2010.

Majumdar, R.C, *History of Modern Bengal, Part one (1765-1905),* G. Bharadwaj & Co., Calcutta, 1978.

Mukherjee, B.N. (ed.), *Early Historical Perspective of North Bengal*, N.B.U., 1987.

Nag, Hiten (ed.), *Cooch Beharer Itihas*, N.L.Publisher, Siliguri, 2005.

Nag, Hiten (ed.), *America through Hindu Eyes*, N.L.Publisher, Siliguri, 2004.

Pal, Joydoop, *The Untold History of the Princely State of Cooch Behar*, Sopan Publisher, Kolkata, 2015.

Pal, Joydeep, *The multi avenues of revenue management and settlement operation system in Cooch Behar – A study of the monarchical achievement*, Sopan Publisher, Kolkata, 2015.

Pal, Joydeep, *The Cooch Behar State and its history of modernity (1839-1950),* Abhijeet Publications, New Delhi, 2017.

Pal, Joydeep, *Glimpses of Cooch Behar State : A model State in Colonial Writings*, Abhijeet Publications, New Delhi, 2019.

Pal, Joydeep, *Legal and Criminal justice under the Cooch Behar Raj (1863 – 1911),* Abhijeet Publications, New Delhi, 2020.

Pal, Joydeep, *History of Revenue and Settlement Operation under the Cooch Behar Raj: From the beginning upto 1912*, Abhijeet Publications, New Delhi, 2021.

Pal, Joydeep, *The Final Farewell*, Sopan Publisher, Kolkata, 2021.

Rhodes, Nicholas & Bose, Shankar. K., *The Coinage of Cooch Behar*, Library of Numismatic Studies, Dhubri, India, 1999.

Sanyal, Charu Chandra, *Rajbansis of North Bengal, Vol. – xi*, Asiatic Society, Calcutta, 1965.

Sanyal, Ratna Roy, *The Raj and the Princely State of Cooch Behar – A* Study of Anglo – Cooch Behar Relations (1772 – 1839), Dipali Publishers, Chanchal, Malda, 2004.

Sarkar, Anil Kumar, *British Paramountcy and the Cooch Behar State*, Abhijeet Publications, Delhi, 2011.

Sarkar, Ichhimuddin, *Aspects of Historical Geography of Pragjyotisa – Kamarupa (Ancient Assam),* Naya Prokash, Calcutta, 1992.

Books (Bengali)

Achrya, Sujit Kumar, *Kam Kamta Kamakhya Tatha koch Rajbansider Dravidio Utshya*, Indiana, Kolkata, 2007.

Ahmed, Amanutullah, *History of Cooch Behar* (in Bengali), Cooch Behar State Press, 1936.

Bandhopadhaya, Amiya Kumar & Das, Sudhir Ranjan (ed.), *Cooch Behar Zillar Purakirti*, Puratattya Bibhag, Government of West Bengal, 1974.

Bandhopadhaya, Tapas Kumar, *Koch O Totoder Samaj Sanskriti*, Pratibhas, Kolkata, 2008.

Bandapadhaya, Bhagavatee Charan, *Cooch Beharer Itihas*, Cooch Behar State Press, Cooch Behar, 1882.

Barma, Hemanta Kumar Roy, *Cooch Beharer Itihas*, Pranati Books, Cooch Behar, Reprint, 2005.

Bhattachariya, Gauri Sankar, *Uttarbanger Pathe Pathe*, Economic Book Stall, Siliguri, 2005.

Bhattacharya, Himadri Sankar, *Cooch Behar O Prachin Prathar Kichu Jana O Ajana Katha*, Madhurima Ofset, Cooch Behar, 2002.

Dalai, Ghanashyam, *Sachitra Kuchbehar - Rajchitra*, Kuntalin Press, Calcutta, 1915

Das, Bhagirath (ed.), *Cooch Behar Loksanskrit Utsav - Smarak Grantha*, Floriculturist Research Institute of Cooch Behar, Cooch Behar, 2001.

Das, Biswanath, *Maharanee Sunity Devi - Coochbehar Maharanee Sunity Devir Jiban*

Katha (in Bengali), Sishu Sahitya Sansad, Calcutta, 2000.

Das, Biswanath (ed.), *Rajopakhyan*, Mala Publications, Calcutta, 1985.

Deb, Ranajit, *Cooch Beharer Itihas*, Delta Farma, Calcutta, 2005.

Deb, Ranajit, *Cooch Beharer Eitijhyamoyee Rajprasad*, Purbottar Prakashan, Calcutta, 1999.

Deb, Saswati, *Cooch Behar Parichaya*, Purbouttar Prakashan,Cooch Behar, 2006.

Debnath, Mahendra, *Shahar Cooch Beharer Tinsha Bachar*, Vikash Publishar, Kolkata, 2007.

Debnath, Mahendra, *Atmakathane Cooch Behar Maharani Brindeswari o Jenkins School*, Lekhapara Publisher, Cooch Behar, 2010.

Devi, Brindeswari, *Beharodanta*, Kakiniyastha Printer,Cooch Behar, 1859.

Dey, Dilip Kumar, *Cooch Beharer Lokosanskriti*, Anima Prakashani, Calcutta, 2007.

Ghosh, Ananda Gopal & Das, Nilangshu Sekhar, *Uttar Banger Itihas o Samaj*, Dipali Publisher, Malda, 2009.

Halder, Sashibhusan, *Cooch Behar Hitaishinee Sabha Baktritamala*, Cooch Behar, 1965.

Majumdar, Arun Bhusan, *Pratyush O Pradosh Kaler Kamta - Cooch Behar*, Arya Publishing House, New Delhi, 2008.

Majumdar, Shubhendu, *Adhunik Siksha O Cooch Behar Victoriya College (1888 – 1938)*, West Bengal state Book Board, 2000.

Pal, Joydeep, *Oitijhyabahi Cooch Beharer Itihaser Ruprekha, Progressive* Publisher, Kolkata, 2016.

Paul, Nripendra Nath, *Itikathay Cooch Behar*, Anima Prakashani, Kolkata, 2000.

Paul, Nripendra Nath (ed.), *Koch Kings of Kamrup*, Anima Prakashani, Calcutta, 1985.

Paul, Nripendra Nath (ed.), *Maharaj Harendra Narayan O Shibendra Narayaner Bhaktigiti Sangraha*, Anima Prakashani, Kolkata, 1999.

Ray, Schindra Nath, *Sahitya Sadhanaya Rajanya Shasita Koch Behar*, Suprime Publishers, Kolkata, 1999.

Ray, Swapan Kumar, *Prachin Koch Beharer Sampurna Itibritta*, Baiwala, Kolkata, 2006.

Ray, Swapan Kumar, *Prachin Koch Beharer Aartho- Samajik Itihas*, Baiwala, Kolkata, 2008.

Ray, Swapan Kumar, *Kochbihar Rajdarabarer Sahityacharcha*, Books Way Publisher, Kolkata, 2011.

Roy, Abhijit, *Koch Behar Raj-Jnankosh (1510 – 1949)*, Anima Prakashani, Kolkata, 2002.

Sanyal, Soven, *Alipurduarer Pathe Prantare*, Alipurduar Nature Club, Alipurduar Court, 2006.

Sanyal, Soven, *Cooch Behar Kichu Katha, Kichu Itihas*, Alipurduar Nature Club, Alipurduar Court, 2008.

Sarkar, Abhijit, *Cooch Beharer Chithi*, Cooch Behar Press, Cooch Behar, 2004.

b) Unpublished Ph.D Dissertations :

1) Das, Kamalesh Chandra, "Modernisation of a Princely State Cooch Behar under the Maharaja Nripendra Narayan (1863 – 1911)", Department of History, University of North Bengal.
2) Sen, Partha Kumar, "Study of some aspects of the history of Kamata Cooch Behar since 1772 to the date of Accession of Shivendra Narayan", Department of History, University of North Bengal.
3) Sircar, Sekhar, "Land Settlement and Revenue Administration and taxation under the Maharajas of Cooch Behar State, (1773 – 1949)", Department of Economics, University of North Bengal.

c) Journals, Magazines, News Papers

1) Achrya, Nirmalya (ed.), *Ekkhan, 1995-96.*
2) *Bengal past & Present* – 2002.
3) Bhattachariya, Ajitesh (ed.), *Madhuparni,* Vol. of Cooch Behar (ed.) by Ananda Gopal Ghosh, August, 1990.
4) Bhattachariya, Aninda & Biswas, Rajarshi (ed.), *Manshai,* (2007 & 2008).
5) Chaki, Debabrata (ed.), *Uttar Prasanga* – Vol. –1,2,3 (2008).
6) Das, Sukhendu (ed.)- Cooch Behar Zilla Sankha, Dept. of information & Culture, Govt. of West Bengal, July, 2006.

7) *Smaranika* (Dinhata Municipality), Cooch Behar, 4 th Oct., 2002.

8) *Smaranika* (Jenkins School), 2011.

9) *Smaranika* (Khudra Patra- Patrika Parishad), Uttar Banga, 17-19, Dec, 2010.

10) *Smaranika* (North Bengal State Library), Cooch Behar, 1996.

11) *Smaranika* (Sunity Academy), 1981, 2006.

12) *Uttarbanga Sambad,* 17th, August, 2008.

■■■■